Ironies Leaders Navigate

Ironies Leaders Navigate

What the Science of Power Reveals
about the Art of Leadership and
the Distinct Art of Church Leadership

SECOND EDITION

SCHUYLER TOTMAN

RESOURCE *Publications* • Eugene, Oregon

IRONIES LEADERS NAVIGATE, SECOND EDITION
What the Science of Power Reveals about the Art of Leadership and the Distinct Art of Church Leadership

Copyright © 2018 Schuyler Totman. All rights reserved. Except for brief quotations in critical publications or reviews, no part of this book may be reproduced in any manner without prior written permission from the publisher. Write: Permissions, Wipf and Stock Publishers, 199 W. 8th Ave., Suite 3, Eugene, OR 97401.

Resource Publications
An Imprint of Wipf and Stock Publishers
199 W. 8th Ave., Suite 3
Eugene, OR 97401

www.wipfandstock.com

PAPERBACK ISBN: 978-1-5326-4042-1
HARDCOVER ISBN: 978-1-5326-4043-8
EBOOK ISBN: 978-1-5326-4044-5

Manufactured in the U.S.A.   APRIL 10, 2018

Scripture verses taken from the Holy Bible, New International Version®, NIV®. Copyright © 1973, 1978, 1984, 2011 by Biblica, Inc.™ Used by permission of Zondervan. All rights reserved worldwide. www.zondervan.com The "NIV" and "New International Version" are trademarks registered in the United States Patent and Trademark Office by Biblica, Inc.™

Dedicated to
Mary Harrison Totman

Contents

Introduction: Five Caveats | ix

    CHAPTER 1   A Redeeming Look at Power | 1

A First Look at . . .
    CHAPTER 2   Many Definitions of Power | 9
    CHAPTER 3   Myriad Forms of Power | 15
    CHAPTER 4   Myriad Purposes for Power | 27
    CHAPTER 5   Power as Constant and Relational | 33

A Longer Look at . . .
    CHAPTER 6   Endorsement | 43
    CHAPTER 7   Other People's Power: Six Orientations | 60
    CHAPTER 8   Dependence | 74
    CHAPTER 9   Face and Identity | 80
    CHAPTER 10   Trust and Distrust | 98
    CHAPTER 11   Different Forms of Authority | 112
    CHAPTER 12   The Ironies of Coercive Power | 125
    CHAPTER 13   The Ironies of Power Imbalance | 132

Bibliography | 149

Introduction: Five Caveats

> Leadership is intentional influence.
> —*Michael McKinney*

> Power is "deliberate influence."
> —*Morton Deutsch*

Here is, foundationally, a glossary. This brief book presents about sixty studied terms and definitions which help us examine the nebulous subject of power. These concepts serve as lenses through which to study leadership settings, because it turns out that leadership and power have almost everything in common. Definitions of power and definitions of leadership, even as they vary and increase in complexity beyond the two above, keep saying the same things. Chapter 2 will demonstrate this by comparing 10 definitions of each. For every respected definition of leadership, you can find a respected definition of power that makes the same statement. Hence every act of leadership is an act of power, and the better we understand power, the better we understand leadership. This book offers that basic but better understanding of power, in part by illustrating these studied terms within everyday leadership settings.

INTRODUCTION: FIVE CAVEATS

However, while its methods and objective are straight-forward, this book merits several caveats. First, I shouldn't suggest that it's an easy read, in part because power is an uneasy topic, as Chapter 1 addresses. Also, this book will complicate terms we use with familiar ease, like power, authority, dependence, trust and distrust. Those reading further should be prepared to never again see these terms as simple or separate. This book will fragment them and then weave their pieces together with others.

For example, dependence will be dissected into **voluntary dependence**, a dynamic more commonly recognized as trust, and **involuntary dependence**, a necessary ingredient for the absolute power Lord Acton warns us about. Trust itself will be parsed into **calculus-based trust** (CBT) and **identification-based trust** (IBT), and these will be studiously compared and connected to differing forms of distrust. **Given authority** will be distinguished from other forms of authority, and the four sources of given authority will be contrasted.

A second caveat about this book is that, while it provides lenses to help understand any leadership setting, it is written with a particular leadership setting in mind, the local church. But this setting is best explored by studying how power clarifies leadership settings in general, and then contrasting how this setting is distinct. **Those pages framed by lined boxes address this setting specifically**. The first of these pages appears at the end of this preface, and the rest appear at the ends of chapters 6 and beyond.

In short, most of this book is written for the benefit of all leaders, but all of it is written for the benefit of church leaders.

A third caveat: if studying power helps to clarify leadership settings, it does not help to simplify them. Examining leadership through the lenses of power is like holding an X-ray up to flat light or examining a petri dish under a microscope. The simple becomes complex. Latent factors become defining. Studying power takes some of the romance out of leadership. But it does replace it elsewhere.

Still, these terms and definitions merely name what leaders already feel. This study of power does not really offer anything new

INTRODUCTION: FIVE CAVEATS

about leadership settings, but instead names and identifies instinctive challenges, joys and stressors already experienced by leaders and those they seek to lead.

Fourth, studying the power inherent in leadership reveals many ironies. But the term *irony*, like power, is one name for many concepts. The ironies presented here are *situational* ironies, falling under the definition: "A situation that is strange or funny because things happen in a way that seems to be the opposite of what you expected."[1] One example of situational irony is, "If you have a phobia of long words you have to tell people that you have Hippoptomonstrosesquipedaliophobia?"[2] Another example is a *pyrrhic victory*, one so costly that it leaves the victor effectively defeated. It should be noted that ironies are to some degree artistic and subjective, based as they are on expectations and assumptions. One person may find something ironic that another does not, and some ironies are more ironic than others.

Many of the ironies described here should be familiar to leaders. Some, like *the irony of Al Capone* and *the ironies of given authority*, are inevitable. They just describe how it is for leaders. Others, like *the consumer's irony*, are effectively unavoidable. Some leaders might consider *the mentor's irony* and *the irony of trusting distrust* ideal; symptoms of effective, empowering leadership. And some of these ironies, such as *the terrorist's irony* and *the double irony of the coercive leader*, are both self-imposed and self-defeating. While this book does it's best to remain objective, the study of power does reveal some good examples of bad leadership.

These ironies lead to a final caveat, and why this book should be brief, and should not be an "easy read." Leadership is not the work of studying concepts and definitions. Rather, leadership is a work of art. As Dwight D. Eisenhower advised, "Leadership is the art of getting someone else to do something you want done because he wants to do it." Michael McKinney furthers this perspective:

---

1. *Merriam-Webster Online*, "irony."
2. Isitironic.com, "Examples of Irony."

INTRODUCTION: FIVE CAVEATS

> To reduce leadership to a set of algorithms is to remove it from its context; to ignore the complexities, the contradictions, and the possibilities. Artists must deal with uncertainty, contradictions and diversity almost by definition. Leaders need to have this capacity."[3]

The terms presented here name these complexities and possibilities, but do not reduce or control them. And the ironies merely encapsulate the uncertainty, contradictions, and diversity encountered in leadership settings.

Much more could be written about every concept and dynamic presented here, but this might actually interfere with the objective. The hope is that this book helps leaders better appreciate their power, resulting in the wise, constructive use of it in ways that come naturally to each.

In short, this book does its best to not be a *how-to* book. Robert Greenleaf warns that servant leadership must not be a deliberately undertaken "gimmick," but rather an inner drive to "just be it."[4] Similarly, each leader's use of power must be authentic and artistic.

SHOULD WE TALK ABOUT POWER IN CHURCH?

Understanding power helps to differentiate the artistic challenges faced within different leadership settings. The "complexities, contradictions and possibilities" of leadership within an accounting firm, for example, differ from those within a public middle school. The impetus for this book was a better understanding of a particular leadership setting—the local church.

Church leaders, just like The Church's Leader, navigate all the power-related challenges other leaders experience, and a few more (for a partial list, see p. 54). But appreciating those challenges unique to this setting requires a circuitous approach. This book examines some of what power reveals about leadership in

---

3. McKinney, "Leading Thoughts."
4. Greenleaf, *Power of Servant Leadership*, 145.

general, and then, by comparison and contrast, some of what it reveals about The Church and its leader, Jesus Christ, and only then explores some of the distinct challenges and opportunities local church leaders face.

And these are significant, enough so to bring leadership guru Peter Drucker to conclude that certain church leadership settings were at once both highly successful, and nevertheless "the most difficult job" he had ever studied.[5]

Those not intrigued by distinct challenges faced within local churches, and within The Church, can pass over those pages framed in lined boxes, like the next one. The rest appear after chapter 5. (Note: A few examples of power dynamics from Scripture will be used outside these boxes, because they are simply too illustrative to pass by.)

5. Sjogren, "ChurchPlanting.com."

Introduction: Five Caveats

On power and Power in church and The Church

But isn't the local church, and The Church, about the Power of God, rather than mere human power? As Paul states:

> "My message and my preaching were not with wise and persuasive words, but with a demonstration of the Spirit's power, so that your faith might rest not on men's wisdom, but on God's power." (1 Corinthians 2:4)

Agreed, and the better we understand power, the better we understand Power. The two often work the same, and very often work together. Consider how Christ embeds the former within the latter:

> [But] you will receive power when the Holy Spirit comes on you; and you will be my witnesses in Jerusalem, and in all Judea and Samaria, and to the ends of the earth. (Acts 1:8)

> And I tell you that you are Peter, and on this rock I will build my church, and the gates of Hades will not overcome it. (Matthew 16:18)

Understanding power helps us recognize a) those miraculous instances in which Power works apart from power, b) those edifying instances in which power works under Power, and c) those faithless, unnecessary, sometimes egregious instances in which power works alone, apart from Power.

Studying power also helps us appreciate how Jesus leads. This includes how he usually confines himself to mere social power, refusing to overwhelm with divine Power, even when tempted in the wilderness, even when facing the cross. The parables he creates are all very human means of influence. (Every concept this book presents could be illustrated within the parable of the prodigal son.) In short, Jesus works hard to not *over*power.

Finally, Jesus' interactions with his followers—e.g. absorbing Martha's tirade in Luke 10; observing the disciples' running "who's the greatest" argument (see Luke 9 and 22)—provide some of the most humorous, and human, examples of power dynamics available.

CHAPTER 1

A Redeeming Look at Power

HOW EXACTLY ARE LEADERSHIP AND POWER RELATED?

The answer to this question presents itself when definitions of each are placed adjacent. Consider three pairings as examples:

> Power is deliberate or purposive influence.
>
> —*Morton Deutsch*

> Leadership is intentional influence.
>
> —*Michael McKinney*

> [Power is] the ability to bring about desired outcomes.
>
> —*Peter T. Coleman*

> Leadership is the capacity to translate vision into reality.
>
> —*Warren Bennis*

> By social power we mean an individual's potentiality for influencing one or more other persons toward acting or changing in a given direction.
>
> —George Levinger

> Leadership is the art of getting someone else to do something you want done because he wants to do it.
>
> —Dwight D. Eisenhower

The words in each pair differ, but the meanings remain the same. This essential resemblance between leadership and power persists, even as definitions of power and definitions of leadership vary from one another and increase in complexity. Chapter 2 demonstrates this further by comparing 10 respected definitions of each. Two conclusions can be drawn from this resemblance. First, every act of leadership is an act of power. Second, the better we understand power, the better we understand leadership.

And we misunderstand power, scholars lament in a varied chorus, in part by under-understanding power. Dacher Keltner, in *The Power Paradox*, describes how our recognition of power is often confined to "businessmen initiating hostile takeovers" and "bullies on the middle-school playground tormenting smaller kids."

Beyond under-understanding power, we understand power differently, as the varied definitions above illustrate. Given all this, the basic purpose of this book emerges: expand our understanding of leadership by addressing the ways we misunderstand, under-understand and understand differently the power intrinsic to leadership.

Exploring power does indeed reveal much about leadership. Power, including the many forms it takes and the many dynamics that shape it, has been studied in careful detail. Even a basic overview shines a bright, almost clinical light on leadership and leadership settings. Still, the study of power does not offer anything new about leadership. It merely takes a closer look, naming dynamics already felt within leadership settings.

A REDEEMING LOOK AT POWER

THE FIRST IRONY OF POWER IN LEADERSHIP

But before discussing power further, we must address how we generally don't like discussing power. Though definitions of power and leadership are effectively synonymous, and though power is at work whenever leaders lead, "Leadership is always a fascinating topic,"[1] while the open discussion of power is often considered "bad taste,"[2] a sign of a distressed relationship.[3] This irony appears to increase as power increases: Hocker and Wilmot observe how "people who hold high power positions are particularly prone to denying they have or use power."

To be clear, power itself is very attractive. "The overwhelming evidence seems to indicate that the powerful tend to like power, use it, justify having it, and attempt to keep it."[4] Rather, we just don't like talking about power. Andy Crouch, author of *Playing God: Redeeming the Gift of Power*, describes being repeatedly urged to use a less "abrupt and unsettling" term for his subject. Several factors help to explain why people, especially leaders, might resist discussing the power inherent within leadership. For instance, power is the active element within many polarizing dynamics, e.g., *power hungry*, *power struggle*, *political power*, *overpower*, *firepower*. Lord Acton's famous statement, "Power tends to corrupt, and absolute power tends to corrupt absolutely," furthers this notoriety. Others do come to power's defense with arguments like:

> Power doesn't corrupt people, people corrupt power.
>
> —William Gaddis

> There is nothing wrong with power if power is used correctly.
>
> —Dr. Martin Luther King Jr.

---

1. Vecchio, "Introduction and Overview," 1.
2. Kipnis, *Powerholders*, 2.
3. Ury et al., *Getting Disputes Resolved*, 7–8.
4. Coleman, "Power and Conflict," 124.

Yet, even as these statements confront power's bad reputation, they acknowledge that it is very often guilty by association. Power is at its most recognizable in overtly competitive settings like sports, elections, and elimination "reality" shows. These spectacles captivate precisely because they offer dramatic win/lose platforms. Beyond these formal arenas, but perhaps because of them, people often equate power solely with struggle. "In many discussions, the concept of power is linked only to the ability to overcome resistance."[5]

Associating power with opposition also makes sense given power's integral connection with conflict. Power has been called the "architecture"[6] and "structure"[7] of conflict. Indeed this book draws heavily upon the scholarly study of power as it relates to conflict. Conflict situations can be dissected and examined according the sources of power each party controls. Further, the collaborative resolution of conflict often involves parties becoming aware of, redirecting, and even explicitly refraining from using those sources of power available to them.

The association between conflict and power, coupled with the association between power and leadership, exposes a dynamic many leaders already appreciate: leadership often looks and feels like conflict management. In other words, what instance of leadership is *not* an instance of either resolving, or avoiding, or instigating, or, in a word, *managing* conflict? In fact, many definitions distinguishing great leaders from leaders address how great leaders embrace conflict:

> A leader takes people where they want to go. A great leader takes people where they don't necessarily want to go, but ought to be.
>
> —*Rosalynn Carter*

---

5. Deutsch, *Resolution of Conflict*, 87.
6. Folger, et al., *Working Through Conflict*, 136.
7. Hocker and Wilmot, *Interpersonal Conflict*, 105.

> All of the great leaders have had one characteristic in common: it was the willingness to confront unequivocally the major anxiety of their people in their time. This, and not much else, is the essence of leadership.
>
> —*John Kenneth Galbraith*

> Great leaders are almost always great simplifiers, who can cut through argument, debate, and doubt to offer a solution everybody can understand.
>
> —*General Colin Powell*

Power's connection with conflict, competition and coercion helps to explain why leadership seldom conspicuously associates with power, despite their near synonymy. In fact, of the entire "Top 100 Best Quotes on Leadership," as published by *Forbes*, only one mentions power. And this one—Seneca's caution that "He who has great power should use it lightly"—doesn't mention leadership.

A REDEEMING LOOK AT POWER

Despite any bad reputation, "power is neither positive nor negative—power just is."[8] A newborn's first cry is a reflexive effort to *bring about desired outcomes*. Referring to power as bad or good "is akin to classifying our breathing function as good or bad."[9] Confronting the perception that power is equated solely with coercion, Deutsch responds: "This seems too narrow a view. It overlooks the possibility that power can be facilitative as well as coercive, that it can liberate as well as restrain, that it can be 'for' as well as 'against.'"[10]

In short, power is at work when good—great or small—comes from people *purposively influencing* each other. It is, for example, an act of power (and leadership) when:

---

8. Hocker and Wilmot, *Interpersonal Conflict*, 73.
9. Ibid.
10. Deutsch, *Resolution of Conflict*, 87.

- An eight-year-old girl specifies in her birthday party invitation that guests should bring items for the local animal shelter in lieu of gifts.
- The CEO of a capital investment firm closes its doors and ushers staff from Boston to New York City, where they walk the streets and hand out flyers in hopes of finding a coworker's runaway daughter.
- Two college softball players carry the batter from the opposing team around the diamond, lowering her so that she can touch her foot to each base, because she has just torn her ACL hitting a home run against them and can't walk, and the rules state the home run won't count unless she touches the bases and that her own teammates cannot help her.

Power is at work when the President of the United States bends down and allows a five-year-old boy to rub his hair, to confirm that they are like each other. When Jesus Christ tells the parable of the Good Samaritan, every benevolent act ascribed to the main character is an act of power.

Saying "Please" or "You can do it" or "Your way is better" or even "I love you" are acts of power, if they *purposively influence* another, if they work to *bring about desired outcomes*. It is an act of power when a father counts to three and lets go of the bicycle, jogging behind as his five-year-old daughter pedals on alone.

And as their near-synonymous definitions reveal, every act of leadership is an act of power. In all the myriad forms it takes (see chapter 3), power is how leaders *purposively influence* those they strive to *intentionally influence*. Power is the stuff under the hood of leadership. A leader seeking to understand power is like a surgeon examining her instruments before operating, or a pitcher scrutinizing his curve ball on slow-motion video.

Power is the means by which leaders lead.

So what is power, exactly?

A First Look at . . .

Chapter 2

Many Definitions of Power

> As is illustrated by the vast literature on power from philosophy, history, sociology, political science, and psychology, there are about as many conceptualizations of power as there are authors who have written on it.
>
> —*Peter Coleman*

> There are almost as many different definitions of leadership as there are persons who have attempted to define the concept.
>
> —*Bernard Bass*

> Like love, we know that power exists, but we cannot agree on a description of it.
>
> —*David Kipnis*

People recognize social power in widely differing ways. We may equate power with control, authority, expertise, manipulation, money, credibility, sway, strength, charisma, force, persuasion, impact, or leverage. These synonyms vary greatly, but power can be any and all of the above.

Definitions of power appear to fall into three categories, those with an **outcome** or **task emphasis**, those with a **relational emphasis**, and those with a **connection emphasis**, which seek to meld relationships with outcomes. Examples of each are seen in Table 2.1, along with definitions of leadership that resonate with each:

Table 2.1

Power is . . .	*Leadership is . . .*
Outcome or Task Emphasis	
[Power is] the ability to influence or control events. —Folger, Poole, and Stutman	Leadership is the capacity to translate vision into reality. —Warren Bennis
[Power is] the ability to bring about desired outcomes. —Peter T. Coleman	Effective leadership is not about making speeches or being liked; leadership is defined by results not attributes. —Peter Drucker
Power is . . . the ability to achieve a purpose. —Dr. Martin Luther King Jr.	The very essence of leadership is that you have to have vision. It's got to be a vision you articulate clearly and forcefully on every occasion. You can't blow an uncertain trumpet. —Father Theodore Hesburgh
Relational Emphasis	
Power is the ability to change the behavior of others. —Robert Vecchio	Leadership is intentional influence. —Michael McKinney
A person is powerful when he or she has the resources to act and to influence others and the skills to do this effectively. —Morton Deutsch	A leader takes people where they want to go. A great leader takes people where they don't necessarily want to go, but ought to be. —Rosalynn Carter
By social power we mean an individual's potentiality for influencing one or more other persons toward acting or changing in a given direction. —George Levinger	The task of the leader is to get his people from where they are to where they have not been. —Henry Kissinger

MANY DEFINITIONS OF POWER

Outcome–Relational Connection Emphasis	
Power is deliberate or purposive influence. —Morton Deutsch	People buy into the leader before they buy into the vision. —John Maxwell
Power is said to be exercised when changes occur in the target person's behavior that can be attributed to the powerholder's influence and that serve the powerholder's interests and intentions. Furthermore, these changes would ordinarily not have been carried out by the target person. —David Kipnis	Leadership is the art of getting someone else to do something you want done because he wants to do it. —Dwight D. Eisenhower The first responsibility of a leader is to define reality. The last is to say thank you. In between, the leader is a servant. —Max DePree
Individuals have power when they have access to resources that can be used to persuade or convince others, to change their course of action, or to prevent others from moving toward their goals in conflict situations. —Folger, Poole, and Stutman	Never tell people how to do things. Tell them what to do and they will surprise you with their ingenuity. —General George S. Patton
Interpersonal power is the ability to influence a relational partner in any context because you control, or at least the partner perceives that you control, resources that the partner needs, values, desires, or fears. Interpersonal power includes the ability to resist the influence attempts of a partner. —Hocker and Wilmot	

Like the many synonyms for power, these definitions of power contrast greatly. But they don't go quite so far as to contradict. Power can be any and all of the above, and each adds something to the understanding and appreciation of the others. Still, what are the practical effects of these varied perspectives? How might a leader with a task emphasis differ from a leader with a relational emphasis? What might a gifted person who respects Eisenhower's definition of leadership expect from a leader, and what if that leader adheres solely to Hesburgh's definition of leadership?

INDIVIDUAL VERSUS SOCIAL POWER

Social power must be distinguished from individual power. *Individual* or *personal* power, such as Sarah's ability to fly an airplane or Scott's software programming skill, is a person's ability to achieve a purpose *alone*. Almost opposite to this, social power is a person's ability to influence others to accomplish a purpose. Where individual power belongs to that person, "social power stems from relationships among people."[1] Hannah Arendt was referring to social power when she stated, "Power is never the property of an individual; it belongs to a group and remains in existence only so long as the group keeps together." In short, social power is subject to negotiation. For a person to have social power others must endorse it, a pivotal, never-ending process explored further in Chapter 6.

One's individual power can be a resource for her social power. For example, Sarah's skill as a pilot may influence her airline company to employ her, and passengers to board her airplane. Similarly, Scott may draw upon his programming skills as a lead software engineer, but they will not help him as he coaches his son's Little League baseball team.

Leadership is an act of social power that often draws upon specific forms of individual power.

Scholars describe from various angles the tendency to equate social power with individual power. This misperception is reasonable because the two are so closely connected. In fact, even scholars of power seldom distinguish the two. (Note: this book equates power with social power specifically.) Another factor makes this misperception easier: any definition of power that emphasizes

---

1. Folger et al., *Working Through Conflict*, 140.

outcomes (see Table 2.1) encompasses both individual and social power.

DEPENDENCE AND RESISTANCE

The final two definitions of power in Table 2.1 reference two dynamics crucial within leadership settings: *dependence* and *resistance*.

Dependence mirrors power. The power I have in our relationship is a factor of your dependence on me. You can reduce or remove my power by reducing or removing your dependence. An employee can look for a new job, for example, or a user disgruntled at his email provider may switch to another. You can also increase my power by increasing your dependence on me. The sales director who entrusts a major client to an associate increases his dependence upon her. Dependence, including the connection between trust and voluntary dependence, will be examined in greater detail in chapter 8.

Regarding *resistance*, Hocker and Wilmot's definition in Table 2.1 specifies that power is in part *the ability to resist the influence attempts of a partner*. Folger, Poole, and Stutman describe power in part as the ability to *prevent others from moving toward their goals*. In short, resisting power is itself an act of power. Power is exerted when leadership is resisted. This may take the form of a silent refusal to follow directions, quiet inefficiency, face-to-face pushback, or strategic coalition building, such as workers forming a union.

But is resistance to leadership inherently bad or wrong? Many iconic leaders in history—especially U.S. history—are revered wholly or primarily for their resistance to leadership: George Washington, Benjamin Franklin, Gandhi, Harriet Tubman, Martin Luther King Jr., Winston Churchill, Jesus Christ, Abraham Lincoln. All these earned their title as leader at least in part by resisting leadership. Call this leadership-by-resisting-leadership **the Rosa Parks irony**.

POWER > LEADERSHIP

Power and leadership begin to lose their near synonymy in the light of dynamics like dependence and resistance. Power is more than leadership. Power can be used to resist leadership. A leader's power can, but not necessarily must, diminish when those led reduce dependence. Power is at work when those led have *the ability to change the behavior* of their leaders. And ultimately, a leader's power is a factor of how much she is willing and able to depend on the power of those she leads.

CHAPTER 3

Myriad Forms of Power

Phrases like *money is power, sexual power, knowledge is power,* and *the power of love* help to illustrate the myriad forms power can take. A child may say please, for example, to persuade a grandparent to buy her a candy bar, then move into the early stages of a temper tantrum as a backup plan. A TV salesperson may use a thirty-day free trial option plus free delivery and setup to entice a reluctant customer. A "broad range of resources"[1] can be used to *purposively influence* others.

SOURCES OF POWER

As chapter 2 introduced, individuals control sources of power, such money and expertise. These can be used as *social* power resources if another person values them. Many scholars have categorized sources of power into specific types. Two such efforts, Raven and French's **bases of social power** and Hocker and Wilmot's **power currencies**, are informative individually and in how they contrast.

---

1. Folger et al., *Working Through Conflict*, 140.

Bases of Social Power: Raven and French

- **Reward power:** one's capacity to dispense rewards to those who comply with wants or demands. Questions related to reward power include: Is the reward offered valuable? Can the reward be found elsewhere? Is the person offering the reward capable of producing it?

- **Coercive power:** one's capacity to dispense punishments or bring about unwanted outcomes. In many ways this is the mirror image of reward power. Questions related to coercive power include: Are the unwanted outcomes that bad? Can and will this person actually use this power? Is the punishment, or possible unwanted outcome, worth the rewards or the risk?

- **Legitimate power:** e.g., *given* authority. "Those with legitimate power 'have the right to command the target and the target person is obligated to obey.'"[2] Raven and French argue that legitimate power must be accompanied by coercive power.[3]

- **Referent power:** Power derived from being admired or respected, e.g., charisma, a celebrity spokesman.

- **Expert power:** specific skills or expertise. Note that an expert on ocean tides, for example, may be known as an *authority* on the topic. *Perceived* expertise is all that is needed to influence others. A con man may pass himself off as a doctor if he is believed.

- **Informational power:** derived from the effective use of information, including rational argument and persuasion. Also, the ability to control the flow of information.

---

2. Levinger, "Development of Perceptions and Behavior," 83.
3. Forsyth, *Group Dynamics*, 214.

Power Currencies: Hocker and Wilmot

Hocker and Wilmot categorize power sources from a more relational, contextual perspective.

- **Resource control:** What does a person control—e.g., money, pay raise, approval, promotion—that others value? A person may control resources others want to attain, such as rewards, and resources they want to avoid, i.e., punishments.
- **Interpersonal linkages:** Whom do you know? Who are your friends? One person's affection for another gives the latter this form of power. Interpersonal linkages help one attain power through coalition formation.
- **Communication skills:** speaking skills, the ability to articulate and persuade. Also the ability to form bonds with others through love, caring, nurturing, or understanding gestures.
- **Expertise:** some special skill or knowledge. This may be scholarly expertise, or the familiarity a fisherman has of a certain river.

It must be noted that these categorizations are merely descriptive; many sources of power fit into more than one category. For example, if Elizabeth knows where James' car keys are and he doesn't, her resulting power could be defined as expert power, informational power, or resource control. If she offers to tell them where they are if he promises to take the trash out, Raven and French might call this informational power or reward power or coercive power.

Still, categorizing power clarifies leadership settings in numerous ways. A leader may appreciate, for example, the different forms of power available to him to achieve his purposes. A shipping director may recognize his rapport with his employees (interpersonal linkage power) as distinct from the legitimate power bestowed by his position. Also, a leader can better recognize how power is exerted by those she leads. For example, a director may realize how his assistant uses informational power, alerting one manager of news personally while emailing the others later.

Also, differentiating power helps to clarify what forms of power the leader values in those she leads, and what she does not value. That shipping manager, for example, may refer to his employees as "his muscle," intending this as a compliment, but communicating that he values their physical abilities but not their expertise.

TRUST- AND DISTRUST-BASED POWER

Some forms of power—e.g., referent, expertise, reward—are **trust-based**. They require that the person being influenced has "a confident positive expectation regarding another's conduct."[4] A person regarded by others as *an authority* is trusted to have a definitive level of knowledge on that topic.

Some forms of power, such as coercive power, are **distrust-based**, meaning they require the person being influenced "have a confident negative expectation regarding another's conduct."[5] I must believe that you can and will harm my interests, as a means to change my behavior. A state trooper, for example, may deter speeding via her distrust-based authority to write speeding tickets.

Some forms of power may be seen as trust- or distrust-based by different people. For example, if a restaurant manager has the authority to decide who works the preferred tables, a waiter may see this as reward power (trust-based) or coercive power (distrust-based) depending on many factors.

THE IRONY OF AL CAPONE

Leaders often simultaneously control both trust-based and distrust-based forms of power. A basketball coach may have much wisdom to impart, but also have the distrust-based power to bench

---

4. Lewicki and Wiethoff, "Trust, Trust Development, and Trust Repair," 88.
5. Ibid.

a player for bad grades. A math teacher may know her subject (expertise) and how to teach it (communication skills) and have a strong rapport (interpersonal linkage power) with her students, but still use the authority given her to send an unruly student to the office (distrust-based power). This seemingly incongruous yet constant mingling of trust-and distrust-based power, inevitable to formal leadership settings, can be called ***the irony of Al Capone***, after the gangster who efficiently combined trust-and distrust-based power in his advice, "You can get much farther with a kind word and a gun than you can with a kind word alone." This combination of reward and coercive power is familiar in the metaphor of "the carrot and the stick."

Trust and power are distinct but mutually impacting. The trust that exists between two parties enables the use of trust-based power, and the effective use of trust-based power furthers trust. The same mutuality exists between distrust-based power and distrust. Chapter 8 complicates trust further, in part by describing how both trust and distrust come in different forms: ***calculus-based trust***, that trust we place in someone to deliver as expected, and ***identification-based trust***,[6] that trust we place in a friend or someone with whom we identify.

SETTING-BASED POWER

Power currencies and *power bases* describe those sources of social power that individuals can accumulate. Scholars describe other forms of power that, while they can be controlled by individuals, are best appreciated from the contextual standpoint of the group.

Designated Power

This may be the most readily recognized power in everyday life. Organized society relies on designated law enforcement, elected officials, and government agencies. As individuals, we designate

6. Ibid.

power to the employers, teachers, and doctors. "Who gave you this authority?" "Who made you the boss?" Commuters designate power to stoplights, colored lines on the road, and railroad gates. Designated power encompasses legitimate power, while recognizing that it came from the group, and exists to serve the purposes of the group. Note: within this book, legitimate power, given authority specifically, and designated power are regarded as synonymous. Chapter 11 will explore many different forms of authority.

Though leadership roles often come with designated power, designated power comes with several cautions. First, designated power relationships are "inherently unbalanced" and "distributive,"[7] in that one person receives power while others relinquish it. In short, any setting involving designated power, be it a traffic stop, a doctor's appointment, or the United States in the wake of a presidential election, involves a power imbalance. Such settings, in which I perceive that you have much power and I have little or none, are fertile ground for anxiety and consumerism. This is a second caution. Those who perceive they have low power pose a number of subtle, disparate dangers to leadership settings. Some of these are explored in the final chapter.

Third, as Raven and French contend regarding legitimate power, designated power roles are often substantiated by coercive power. A teacher's role may be under-girded ultimately by the authority to send a student to the office, for example, and a department manager may, as a last resort, rely upon his authority to fire an employee. In fact, given authority and coercive power are often so closely associated that they are regarded as synonymous. Police and other law enforcement agencies, for example, are often referred to collectively as *the authorities.*

Normative Power

Normative power is the power to define group norms. Who is normal and who is deviant? What behavior is exemplary, and what is

---

7. Hocker and Wilmot, *Interpersonal Conflict*, 112.

objectionable? Normative power is the power a group has on the individuals who value belonging to it. We use normative power to instill culture. Informal guidance, such as "that's not how we do things around here" and "don't rock the boat" and "you're not acting black enough," illustrate the how normative power works to define culture. Meanwhile, formal declarations like Semper fi, The HP Way, and "We hold these truths to be self evident..." demonstrate normative power used by formal leadership.

Normative power can be brandished by individuals, such as in group initiation rituals, or when a member of the group applies *peer pressure*. Normative power "is based on the obligations that the other has to accept one's influence as a result of social norms governing the relationship."[8] We maintain a wide, dramatic spectrum of terms for those who resist normative power: *rebel, malcontent, deviant, revolutionary, traitor, innovator*. One who "thinks outside the box," or "refuses to accept the status quo" is resisting normative power. The connection between normative power and *shared identity* will be discussed in chapter 9.

Ecological Power

Ecological power can literally set the stage upon which other forms of power are determined within the group. This is the power to, for example, design a courtroom so that the judge is seated above everyone else, to dress the judge in imposing black robes, and to command "All rise" when that judge enters the courtroom. This setting-defining power "entails sufficient control over the other's social or physical environment to permit one to modify it so that the modified environment induces the desired behavior or prevents undesired behavior."[9] Ecological power is the power a leader has to define the setting in which the group assembles, such as when a teacher assigns seats or when a board chairman places a controversial item at the end of the agenda in order to

---

8. Deutsch, *Resolution of Conflict*, 87.
9. Deutsch, *Resolution of Conflict*, 88.

limit discussion. Prisons sometimes exercise ecological power when giving inmates pants that are much too large and no belts, requiring they hold them up while standing, which occupies their hands and hinders their ability to fight.

Setting based forms of power often co-exist with and complement each other. Laws stating who does and does not have the right to vote, to own land, to drive a car, are the result of normative power and ecological power and designated power working in concert.

Designated, normative, and ecological power are often mainly, and sometimes solely, controlled by a group's formal leader. This stated, a new formal leader may step into a role confined by normative and ecological power. Such a leader may hear guidance like "we've always done it this way," "tradition," and "it comes with the territory" when being instructed how to lead.

POWER IMBALANCE—A FIRST LOOK

Some people have more power than others. I may have more expertise than you, where you may have more friends than I do. Power can also be unequal in cumulative ways: one professor may have more expertise and better communication skills than another. And of course power can be used to accumulate more power. A wealthy person may curry favor, i.e., build interpersonal linkage power, with a sizable donation (reward power, resource control power) to a senator's re-election campaign.

Similarly, two people may have the same form of power, but one may be more amplified. Your voice may carry further than mine. I may have a bigger gun than yours. This example illustrates a further important point about power imbalance: technology is a means to increase power by amplifying it. Your sound system may drown out my stereo. The massive blow-up Santa in your yard may draw more attention than the dancing candy canes in my yard.

Power imbalance also results from one person having ***exclusive power***. One boy may have the only baseball bat in the group, or one traveler may be the only one in the group able to speak Italian.

MYRIAD FORMS OF POWER

Formal leaders often have more power than those they lead for all of these reasons: greater access to power; access to exclusive power, especially legitimate power; primary or sole access to designated and ecological power; pivotal say related to normative power. And all these are accompanied by an increased ability to accumulate more power. However, as explored in Chapter 13, *The Ironies of Power Imbalance*, high power does not necessarily mean more power, or enough power. Further, power can actually interfere with goals leaders seek to achieve.

RESISTANCE TO HIGH POWER

Dutch social psychologist Geert Hofstede describes how some cultures resist power imbalance more than others. Hofstede defines power distance as "the extent to which the less powerful members of institutions and organizations within a country expect and accept that power is distributed unequally."

Specifically, Hofstede designates countries like India, Bangladesh, and China as **large power-distance cultures**: people within these settings are more likely to "accept a hierarchical order in which everybody has a place and which needs no further justification." By contrast, in **small power-distance cultures**, like Canada and Austria, power imbalance is more likely to be met with anxiety and efforts to balance power. "In societies with low power distance, people strive to equalize the distribution of power and demand justification for inequalities of power."

These cultures differ greatly in how they view authority. Those within large power-distance cultures accept power imbalance as appropriate. "Hierarchy in [such] an organization is seen as reflecting inherent inequalities, centralization is popular, subordinates expect to be told what to do and the ideal boss is a benevolent autocrat." Meanwhile, those in small power-distance cultures see authority as necessary but open to scrutiny. "Hierarchy is established for convenience, superiors are always accessible and managers rely on individual employees and teams for their expertise."

Beyond the workplace, Ting-Toomey and Chung describe how large power-distance cultures differ from small power-distance cultures in approach to education and family. "In large power distance family situations, children are expected to obey their parents. Children are punished if they talk back or contradict their parents." In small power-distance settings, "children may contradict their parents and speak their mind. They are expected to show self-initiative and learn verbal articulateness and persuasion skills."[10] In small power-distance settings children can be powerful and a child can be a leader. Ting-Toomey and Chung also describe how in large power-distance settings teachers are likely to lecture, while in small power-distance settings teachers are more likely to discuss and ask for feedback.[11]

INFLUENCE > POWER > LEADERSHIP

In the same way that power is more than leadership, influence is more than power. Morton Deutsch makes the important distinction that while "power is *deliberate* or *purposive* influence," "without intending to do so, one may influence another's values, beliefs, or behaviors." A person may be rich, but this is not resource control power until she *uses* that wealth to deliberately change the behavior of another. Others may treat her differently because she is rich, but this endorses her influence, not her power.

The difference between power, influence, and leadership is seen in the distinction between referent influence, referent power, and referent leadership. Sources of referent *influence*—e.g., popularity, celebrity status—become referent *power* only when they are deliberately used to influence others. For example, a football player's ability or personality may afford him some referent influence, causing people to watch him play and perhaps buy replicas of his jersey. If he draws upon this status to hawk a particular car in a TV commercial, this is the purposive use of his status, i.e., referent

10. Ting-Toomey and Chung, *Understanding Intercultural Communication*, 64–65.
11. Ibid.

power. Such instances of referent power are common, but a truly referent, or charismatic, leader is quite rare, "endowed with supernatural, superhuman, or at least specifically exceptional powers or qualities."[12] A referent leader is able intentionally draw upon the devotion of her followers to lead them. Referent leadership, including how the term *follower* is empowering within referent leadership settings, is explored in chapter 9.

SHARED POWER

Power can be shared, such as when one traveler who speaks Italian teaches others in the group how to say "train station," or when the child with the only bat allows other players to use it. But these differing examples illustrate the consequences of sharing different forms of power. When the child shares the bat, for example, this form of resource control power can be taken back. The child can threaten to take his bat and go home if his sister doesn't get to play. A committee treasurer can have her check-writing duties taken away. In contrast, whatever expertise or special skills the traveler shares are forms of power that cannot be unshared.

When power is shared carefully, the total power of the group increases. "With cooperation you actually create more power than the two of you could have created separately. Shared power is not a weak, tentative approach—it is powerful and energetic, and it requires great skill."[13]

CONVERTING ANY POWER TO COERCIVE POWER

One of the reasons power is often equated with coercion is because any form of power can be used coercively. A sales manager may, for example, use her legitimate power in an effort to coerce higher performance, saying, "If numbers don't improve, four of you won't be here next quarter." A wealthy donor to a museum may vocally

---

12. Weber, *On Charisma and Institution Building*, 48.
13. Hocker and Wilmot, *Interpersonal Conflict*, 132.

threaten to stop giving in response to a change in policy. As this example implies, forms of specifically trust-based power, such as expertise or special skills, can be easily converted to coercive, distrust-based power by threatening to withhold them. A football player holding out is threatening to withhold his special skills to coerce a new contract.

These examples illustrate ***the ironies of converted coercion***. First, in all of these cases, power converted to coercive power may be more effective, i.e., more powerful, than that form of power in its pure form. The rich donor, for example, may get her way more effectively by threatening to not give her money than by giving it. A manager threatening termination may improve effort more efficiently than by providing training and support. Second, using any form of power coercively is often simpler and easier than using that form of power in its pure form. The football player who holds out, for example, simply stops doing the dangerous, physically and mentally demanding work he is valued to do.

Coercive power is a factor in many power-related ironies, including a particularly virulent strain of *violent ironies*. These will be explored in chapter 12.

Chapter 4

Myriad Purposes for Power

Power is necessary for every need, want, purpose, concern, goal, etc. we have, from air and food to belonging and validation. Maslow's famous hierarchy of needs is an enduring monument to the constant, ongoing need for power, both individual and social. Consider the following list. Each item is either a goal or a motivation for a goal, and each requires power:

Table 4.1

wants	needs	concerns	desires	ambitions
purposes	purpose	longing	belongings	belonging
interests	intimacy	motives	motivations	esteem
lusts	impulses	anxieties	anxiety	dignity
values	agendas	power	envy	approval
love	preferences	orders	empathy	reputation
loyalty	expectations	peace	obligations	validation
integrity	temptations	promises	meaning	autonomy
objectives	intentions	urges	convenience	respect
fatigue	impatience	duty	priorities	independence
pressure	hopes	hope	entertainment	freedom
thirst	hunger	safety	money	family

This list could be twice as long and still incomplete. Who is not managing, and being managed by, dozens of these at the same time? And any of these that requires relationship requires social power. Further, the items in this list often compete. How often do my immediate wants and impulses win out against my deeper concerns, such as my ideals and hopes? Which section of Table 4.1 is more important: the last row or the last column?

We may recognize some of the items listed in the table in a *prospective* way, meaning they are known before any efforts to achieve them. Or awareness may be *retrospective*, such as when a felt need like hunger reminds me I have not eaten.

DIFFERENTIATING GOALS

Just as definitions of power can be differentiated, and specific forms of power can be differentiated, scholars differentiate the specific needs, wants, purposes, etc. people bring into relationship. (Note: For brevity, the items listed in Table 4.1 will be condensed into five terms: purposes, needs, wants, goals, and concerns.)

Task or **outcome goals** focus on what we are together to accomplish. Task goals are often obvious, measurable and prospective. Increase shareholder value. Beat the other team. Meet Q4 revenue goals.

Most organizations are established to achieve task goals, such as producing airplanes or developing software solutions or providing support to low-income families. While task goals may be formal and recognizable, they can be fleeting and contextual, such as when three people in an elevator move to accommodate a fourth trying to enter.

Relational goals focus on who we want to be to each other. How closely do I want to associate with you? How comfortable are you depending on me? Do you see me as a colleague where I see you as a good friend? Do I love you more than you love me? Am I too intense for your tastes? Do all my questions get on your nerves? Can I borrow some money? Where are you going? Can I come with you?

Relationship goals change as settings change, even within the same relationship. I may like working with you but not like driving to work with you because you read all the street signs out loud. You may enjoy my company but shudder at the idea of having kids with me. Where task goals are often tangible and prospective, relational goals can be harder to identify and more awkward to discuss. Can I say exactly why I like working one person more than another, and can I describe this to each of them? Relationship goals can also be prospective and retrospective. I may want to work with you right up until your take credit for my idea.

Face concerns encompass "the public self-image that every member wants to claim for himself."[1] Face concerns emphasize how we steward each other's self-image as we interact. Am I showing you respect? Did I say "Excuse me" before imposing on you? Am I speaking to you as an equal or talking down to you, causing you to *lose face*? Hence, face concerns are very often retrospective. A person may become aware of her face concerns only when she has experienced face loss, such as when she has been interrupted or *thrown under the bus*. Terms associated with face loss, such as *insulted, disrespected, indignant, demeaned, embarrassed* and *taken for granted* are usually past tense, indicating their retrospective aspect. These alarming terms also imply how face concerns can suddenly and pivotally disrupt leadership settings.

"Face is something that is emotionally invested, and that can be lost, maintained, or enhanced, and must be constantly attended to in interaction."[2] Chapter 9 will differentiate face concerns into **positive face**, my desire to be regarded highly, and **negative face**, my desire to not be imposed upon or constricted.[3]

Identity concerns closely resemble face concerns, in that both focus on how I see myself and how I want to be seen. But face concerns manifest in the moment, often retrospectively. Identity concerns may prospectively drive me through my whole life. My identity is molded by such forces as my need for recognition, my

---

1. Brown and Levinson, *Politeness*, 61.
2. Ibid.
3. Ibid.

ideals, and my character. My identity concerns may lead me to say, "I want to be a doctor when I grow up" and "I want to be the highest paid consultant in the firm," and "You can depend on me."

My identity is a blend of my **social identity concerns**, which ask "How do I want others to see me?" and my **personal identity concerns**, which ask "How do I see myself?" and "Who am I?" "The teenager who says, 'I don't have premarital sex because it violates my beliefs" is giving a clear identity statement."[4] Identity concerns influence most of my decisions, from whom I associate with to my hairstyle to the car I buy to what causes I espouse. In short, my identity goals likely drive my relationship and outcome goals. My identity goals determine whether I want to be a leader, or merely want to be seen as a leader. My identity concerns determine what kind of leader I want to be, and what kind of leader I want leading me, and what kind I don't.

HOW DIFFERENT KINDS OF GOALS COMBINE

Task goals, relational goals, identity goals, and face concerns intertwine in any relational setting. A single ambition, for example, may simultaneously create ongoing task, relationship, and identity goals, and prompt specific face concerns within interactions.

Leadership settings are an intricate, interwoven mesh of goals: individual and group, task and relationship, identity and face, conscious and unconscious. A professor of political science, for example, may simultaneously teach (task), engage her students as she teaches (relational), and prefer her students call her Professor when they address her (identity and face). This title preference in turn serves task and relationship purposes, instantly clarifying for students both the relationship and the outcomes that relationship exists to achieve.

As chapter 2 illustrated, some definitions of leadership emphasize task goals and some emphasize relational goals. This acknowledged, concerns around face and identity may well impact

---

4. Hocker and Wilmot, *Interpersonal Conflict*, 81.

leadership settings more than relational goals and task goals. Chapter 9 addresses this as it looks more closely at concepts like *face threat, face gain, shared identity, culture,* and *normative power.*

LEADERS STEWARD EVERYONE'S GOALS

Here is perhaps the least compelling definition of leadership ever: leaders strategically and purposively steward goals. The leader aggressively balances the goals of the group with the myriad individual goals of each member, including the leader's own. Consider a practical example: the leader who says, "none of you morons leaves this room, even to use the toilet, until we come up with a solution," is much different from the leader who says, "We'll get this. Let's take a 10-minute break and let people stretch their legs. But keep thinking. We need to agree on a solution and move forward by noon."

Further, a good leader must *prospectively* manage goals others recognize only in retrospect. For example, a high school football player being hospitalized for dehydration reflects on the coach much more than the player. Consider another example: the second chapter of *Art of War*, entitled "Waging War," does not address combat, but instead the expense of war, in all forms.[5] This is to say, for the author Tzu the term *waging war* described a military leader counting the costs of war before entering it.

One of the more mundane ways to measure a leader's effectiveness is to assess the sheer volume and variety of goals that she stewards prospectively. Does a particular leader focus exclusively on the task at hand, and ignore or abuse the relationships? Does a leader focus on getting along with those she leads, to the detriment of the bottom line? Does a leader actively steward the face concerns of those he leads, or is he concerned merely with how he wants them to regard him? And how resolutely does a leader steward the healthy and unhealthy purposes of those she leads? Many

---

5. Sun Tzu, *Art of War*, 26–28.

leaders' legacies are stained, not because of their own actions, but because of the unhealthy impulses of individuals they've led.

This constant mix of needs and wants and concerns and goals a leader must steward—group and individual, leader and led, face and task and relationship, immediate and ongoing, healthy and unhealthy—illuminates the daunting depth of Robert Greenleaf's call to servant leadership:

> The servant-leader is servant first. . . . It begins with the natural feeling that one wants to serve, to serve first. Then conscious choice brings one to aspire to lead. That person is sharply different from one who is leader first, perhaps because of the need to assuage an unusual power drive or to acquire material possessions.
>
> The difference manifests itself in the care taken by the servant—first to make sure that other people's highest priority needs are being served. The best test is this: Do those served grow as persons? Do they, while being served, become healthier, wiser, freer, more autonomous, more likely to see themselves as servants?[6]

---

6. Greenleaf, "Servant as Leader," 412.

CHAPTER 5

Power as Constant and Relational

> "Leadership is practiced not so much in words as in attitude and in actions."
>
> —HAROLD S. GENEEN

Power factors into every single interaction between people. "We are constantly influencing the behavior of others and likewise being influenced by them."[1] For example, two male strangers passing in a narrow hallway may instinctively catch one another's eye and nod their heads slightly, both as a greeting and as way of assuring, "I mean you no harm." No words are exchanged and perhaps only a second elapses, but both parties influence each other, and important purposes are achieved. In a contrasting example, a young female passing a male stranger in the same hallway may well look down and avoid eye contact, fearing she may *send the wrong message*. "Relationships are defined and redefined with every message that speakers send. As a result, relational moves are second nature."[2]

---

1. Steinke, *How Your Church Family Works*, 121
2. Folger et al., *Working Through Conflict*, 155.

POWER IS NEGOTIATED BEYOND WORDS

"While most people dislike discussions of their own power, one cannot avoid using power."[3] Understanding how power is exerted requires understanding the different levels on which we communicate. "Messages have a report aspect that conveys the content of the statement and a command aspect that carries relational messages."[4] **Relational-level messages** involve such elements as tone of voice, volume, emphasis, and body language. The phrase "actions speak louder than words" encapsulates how we give more credence, i.e. more power, to this relational level when we communicate than to what is merely stated on the content level.

Relational messages declare how the one communicating sees the relationship itself, or would like to see it. Consider the example of one person saying to another, "Sit down." This statement has one meaning on a report level, but how many different ways can these words be said relationally? Each communicates how the one speaking views the relationship, or wants to view it, and each is an effort to influence the relationship.

What is communicated on a relational level when a person rolls her eyes, or arrives at a meeting late, or checks her text messages during a presentation she is giving? The relational-level messages embedded within any interaction declare, "I see us as having this kind of relationship."[5]

The challenge within written communications is that the relational-level messages like these are either missing or at least greatly reduced. Relational-level messages involved in a reply email, for example, may be limited to interpreting the choice of words used and how quickly the reply was sent. The power dynamics within an ancient speech, or dialog described in a book, may be subject to much interpretation. One actor may speak the words of Hamlet, for example, very differently than another.

---

3. Hocker and Wilmot, *Interpersonal Conflict*, 96.
4. Folger et al., *Working Through Conflict*, 154.
5. Ibid.

POWER IS CONSTANTLY NEGOTIATED

"During any face-to-face interaction, people constantly define and redefine their relationship."[6] As chapter 2 introduced, social power must be endorsed. Given this, "relational messages are always bids. They attempt to define a certain type of relationship. But they may or may not be successful depending on the listener's response."[7] Do you agree that I have the expertise to guide you? Are you swayed by my confidence? Will the sanctions I impose deter you?

Relational bids can also be communicated without interacting face to face. One person may not return another's voice mail, or *give her the cold shoulder*. A VP may attempt a *power play* by making a job candidate wait thirty minutes in the lobby for a scheduled interview. That candidate may renegotiate the relationship by leaving after fifteen minutes.

Relational-level messages illustrate the fleeting, nuanced ways power works in relationships. Power and influence *are* different—influence can be unintentional. But the instinctive, second-nature quality of relational messages reveals just how fine the line is between power and influence. Power is purposive influence, but the purposes achieved can be subtle, even unconscious. Geneen's admonishment underscores how much leadership plays out on the relational level: "Leadership is practiced not so much in words as in attitudes and actions."

POWER IS EASILY MISINTERPRETED

Relational messages themselves cause problems because they "can be easily denied, misinterpreted or reinterpreted."[8] Simply looking someone in the eye, for example, may indicate trust, agreement, wariness, or threat. An introvert might be seen by others in a group as aloof, when he is actually deeply engaged. Consider a more comprehensive example: if I am looking to *pick a fight*, I

6. Ibid.
7. Ibid.
8. Ibid., 124.

might choose to reinterpret any message you send, regardless of your intent, to achieve my own desired outcomes.

One such form of misinterpretation, that can cripple leadership settings, is called a *fundamental attribution error*:

> The fundamental attribution error occurs when we overestimate how much another person's behavior can be explained by dispositional factors. It reflects failing to adequately consider the role of some situational factors that may affect a person's behavior.[9]

Consider an example: if I am speeding and weaving through traffic with crying kids in the car, I am justified because we are late for a soccer game and time just got away from me. If somebody else is doing the same thing, she is a reckless jerk, and obviously a bad parent in general. When I commit a fundamental attribution error, I attribute another person's behavior to her character, where the same behavior on my part would be justified by my circumstances.

An example of a fundamental attribution error in a leadership setting is a manager calling a worker *dead weight*, attributing her low production numbers to laziness, where the employee sets this pace to insure safety and quality. That same employee may call her manager a *slave driver* based on her repeated demands to work faster, not knowing that the manager has been ordered to let go any workers not performing at a certain pace.

A Deliberate Error?

Fundamental attribution errors are often reactions to observations. But the *picking a fight* example demonstrates how misinterpretations and reinterpretations can be deliberate. A **deliberate** or **convenient attribution error**, though an oxymoron, aptly describes how I can reinterpret another's relational messages in ways that achieve my purposes. A patient sternly advised to stop smoking by his doctor, for example, may label her a "pushy young thing" as a way to disregard her facts and expertise. An elected official may be

9. Psychology and Society, '"Fundamental Attribution Error."

called a moron, though she was intelligent enough to garner election to her office multiple times by a majority of her constituents. Statements like "He's just jealous" or "She's a goody two-shoes" or "He's voting with his wallet" may well be a convenient way to diminish or dismiss another's relational influence by giving him a negative label.

Inversely, I may be just as inclined to rationalize, justifying my own behavior as based on my circumstances rather than my character, seeing my way as right regardless of my motives. Statements like "I was tired when I said that" or "I was just kidding around" can be means to reinterpret or even deny the relational messages I send.

Attribution errors—be they fundamental and unintentional or convenient and deliberate—merit at least two cautions. First, they usually attack another person's identity. They reduce that person into one, small, often terrible force. "She's just a goody two-shoes." They can show that person in the worst light possible, and only that light. In this way, they can dehumanize a person. Consider the implications of calling someone a *fence sitter*, or *dead weight*, a *moron*, or *evil*. Very often, attribution errors are sweeping assessments of character based on one specific action. A second caution is that they justify a competing resistance to that person's efforts. If I can find one fault with what you are trying to do, or how you are trying to do it, or just you, I can resist the whole, perhaps furthering my own identity in the process.

OBLIGATIONS AND EXPECTATIONS

Obligations, be they in the form of responsibilities, pledges, promises, duties, debts, implied agreements or unstated commitments, transfer power from one party to another. If a lawyer agrees to represent a client, for example, she devotes her expertise to achieve his purposes. If I promise to pick you up from the airport, I commit the resources I control (time, driving ability, vehicle) to achieve your purposes.

Expectations travel in the opposite direction as obligations, and they travel light. Expectations are perceived obligations: consciously stated or semi-consciously assumed transfers of power to the person with the expectation. If I expect you to pick me up from the airport, I perceive that the sources of power you control are obligated on my behalf. Ideally in leadership settings, expectations and obligations match, and are consciously agreed upon.

Expectations do not automatically produce obligations, and vice versa. My expectation that you are at the airport does not obligate you to be there. This acknowledged, agreeing to expectations may be as subtle as not overtly resisting them. If you have picked me up the last dozen times, I may assume you are obligated if I simply tell you when my flight gets in. If I am on the same flight every week, no communication may even be necessary for such an expectation to exist; that's how we've always done it. An unrealistic expectation can become a perceived or legitimate obligation simply because agreement is not negotiated. The Latin phrase *Qui tacit consentire* means "Silence implies consent."

Just as expectations do not make obligations, obligations do not make expectations. I may obligate myself to meet your needs or solve your problems without your agreement. Am I trying to *put you in my debt, score points,* or *be a hero*? In other words, am I seeking to further my own identity by meeting your needs? One party obligating himself to all the expectations another just might place upon him would be as unrealistic as that person expecting him to meet all her needs, wants, and desires just because she has them.

POWER AT A DISTANCE

Some relational messages are intended to communicate power at a great distance. A policeman's uniform, the stars on a general's collar, or a sign in the parking lot saying, "Reserved for the Director" are all relational messages designed to communicate across space, "I see us having this kind of relationship." From the perspective of goals discussed in chapter 3, task, relationship, and identity goals can all be communicated at a distance. Flashing lights atop an ambulance are a powerful relational message to nearby drivers on a task, relationship, and identity level.

But if these messages communicate power at a distance, then these messages are subject to interpretation, mis-interpretation and endorsement at the same distance. Consider the range of strong responses, for example, to a police uniform: "The psychological and physical impact of the police uniform should not be underestimated. Depending on the background of the citizen, the police uniform can elicit emotions ranging from pride and respect, to fear and anger."[10] To put this into a practical example, a uniformed police officer walking down a street may cause a group of young men two blocks away to back out of sight and avoid her: at least one of them might be guilty of something. But perhaps this group includes the young man the officer is hoping to find so that she can get him to the hospital to see his mother before her emergency surgery. Still, the young men face two widely contrasting options: risk allowing her to approach them, or maintain a safe distance. Which of these options is the safest, especially given that coercive power, power imbalance, and potential guilt are involved?

OTHER PEOPLE'S POWER—6 WAYS WE SEE IT

One person's power, individual or social, is very often measured on a scale relative to other people's power. Widely varying terms like *fast learner* and *third place* and *gregarious* and *old school* all assess one person's ability to achieve a purpose by comparing it to others'. How does my perception of your power impact my perception of my power?

Depending on many factors, I may have one or more of the following instinctive orientations toward your power.

A ***comparing*** orientation assesses one person's power relative to another's, and is heard in relative terms like *above average*, *middle class*, and *highly experienced*. A job candidate's resume or

---

10. Johnson, "Psychological Influence of the Police Uniform."

a high school student's standardized test scores are both means to compare that person's *ability to achieve a purpose* to others'.

As chapter 1 describes, power is very often recognized from a ***competing*** orientation. This orientation is also comparing, but from an either/or, win/lose perspective: one person's gain means another person's loss. This orientation is familiar in sports and other settings involving finite outcomes. The reverse is also true: a perception of finite outcomes may well prompt a competing orientation. For example, someone with a "chronic competitive perspective on power"[11] may perceive any setting through a win/lose lens. Who is the smartest? Who has the best front lawn? Who is right and therefore who must be wrong?

A ***collaborating*** orientation perceives that my power may increase while yours also increases, or at least that you increasing power doesn't mean my loss. This orientation encompasses teamwork and win/win situations.

Coaches, mentors and teachers have an expansive orientation to others' power. If I have this orientation toward you, my relationship with you exists to increase your power. Your increased power accomplishes my objectives. I am more powerful because I have helped you become more powerful. A ***designated*** orientation recognizes power given to one person by others for the benefit of the group. This is the orientation players have toward a referee and a jury has toward a judge. It is often recognized in familiar terms like *given authority*, *elected office*, and *public service*.

A ***sufficient/insufficient*** orientation instinctively assesses one person's ability to achieve objectives valued by another. Do I trust your ability to do what I need you to do? Do I assume you are capable or incapable related to the task we are performing together? This orientation has a task focus, contrasting to the previous orientations, which are relationally focused.

All of these orientations assess how one person's power impacts another person's power. These six instinctive orientations, including how all can occur in the same relationship, and how each makes for a very different kind of leader, are explored further in chapter 7.

---

11. Coleman et al., *Handbook of Conflict Resolution*, 122.

A Longer Look at . . .

CHAPTER 6

Endorsement

> In systems thinking it is an axiom that every influence is both cause and effect. Nothing is ever influenced in just one direction.[1]
>
> —PETER SENGE

> Being powerful is like being a lady. If you have to tell people you are, you aren't.
>
> —MARGARET THATCHER

Social power differs fundamentally from individual power. As chapter 2 introduced, individual power is a person's ability to achieve a purpose alone, while social power involves the ability to purposively influence others. Hence, where individual power belongs to that person, "[social] power is the property of the relationship rather than the quality of the individual."[2] Familiar phrases like "Michelle has a lot of power in the math department" and "Senator Talbert has the most influence on the committee" are misleading, implying that a person who *has* social power possesses that power. This understanding adheres to a misperception "that power flows in one

---

1. Senge, *Fifth Discipline*, 75.
2. Hocker and Wilmot, *Interpersonal Conflict*, 116.

direction (usually from the top down) and that individuals with differing levels of power do not mutually influence each other."[3]

"Many theorists who have been concerned with power have focused on it solely as an attribute of the actor. This neglects its relational aspects and implicitly assumes that it remains constant across situations, an assumption that is clearly false."[4] "It is critical to bear in mind that power is context-dependent and that even the most powerful people are powerless under certain conditions."[5]

NO ENDORSEMENT, NO POWER

Leadership is as an act of social power and social power is determined within the relationship process. Folger, Poole, and Stutman encapsulate this process in the term ***endorsement***.

> If power stems from relationships, it is misleading to try to identify a particular person who holds power. The more important question may be who assents to the use of power or who withholds endorsement.[6]

Endorsement can take place quickly or slowly, verbally or nonverbally, formally or informally. Endorsement may be clear and specific, such as a Marine private saying "Sir, yes, sir," a colleague clicking the "Endorse" button on a professional networking website, or an audience clapping after a performance. But endorsement is often subtle and silent, accomplished entirely on a relational level. Actively listening or nodding, or sitting when motioned to sit, or just doing what I am told to do endorses. Not doing something you want to when another calls for restraint, such as a stock manager adhering to his company's code of ethics when he has many lucrative reasons not to, is an act of endorsement. The previous chapter described how relational-level messages are bids for power. But they are also means to endorse someone else's power.

3. Coleman and Deutsch, *Handbook of Conflict Resolution*, 112.
4. Deutsch, *Resolution of Conflict*, 85.
5. Coleman and Deutsch, *Handbook of Conflict Resolution*, 124.
6. Folger et al., *Working Through Conflict*, 166.

Further, endorsement is one specific point in an ongoing process. A teenager may complain about doing her chores more loudly than she did when she was eight. On a larger scale, a nation may tolerate imperial leadership for centuries, and then begin to fight for democracy.

To explore the endorsement process in more flowing detail, consider a simple, straight-forward leadership setting, and how the ongoing process of endorsement ultimately defines that setting:

> Some people have gathered to help their friend Eric move out of his apartment. Anne Marie climbs up into the back of the rented truck, and turns to face the others. She declares confidently that she has moved three times before and is an authority on how to load moving trucks. She then instructs them to start by bringing her the heavy boxes first.

Anne Marie's leadership is not established at this point, nor would it be if she repeated herself forcefully. Despite her certainty and her clearly articulated vision and her measurable action steps, she is not the leader yet. Instead, a variety of endorsement-related responses must unfold.

Some may head off to find heavy boxes because they trust her confidence in her own expertise, i.e., they endorse her as *speaking with authority*. Others endorse her clarity and head off as well.

But someone may *negotiate endorsement*, asking, "Shouldn't we load the piano first?" Somebody else may ask almost the same question, but in a significantly different way: "Shouldn't we bring you the piano first?" This question specifically endorses her legitimate power, agreeing that she is the official truck loader, but negotiates endorsement of her expert power. Someone may *withhold* endorsement of Anne Marie's bid for leadership, saying, "Tell us your plan." Someone else may *deny* endorsement: "That's not the right way to do it. Get out of the truck." This response denies endorsement from a task and behavioral perspective. Someone else may deny endorsement in a way that causes face-loss: "You don't know what you're talking about. Step down."

Others may partially endorse Anne Marie, bringing out whatever they find first and setting it down near the truck. In so doing they are relationally parsing Anne Marie's power while furthering the group's task. Some may work slowly, endorsing Anne Marie's leadership but not motivated by it. Some may not endorse her leadership simply because they didn't hear what she said.

From a face perspective, one person may resent Anne Marie's implication that she knows more than he does. Another may perceive the abrupt, eager way she takes charge as merely an attempt to further her own identity goals. These two may jointly make up identity-chiding names for her like *Ruler of the Rental* and *Trucktator*.

Some movers (Eric has many friends and much stuff) may head into the house intending to endorse her leadership, but get caught up in conversation and not bring Anne Marie anything. And finally, two movers may calmly endorse Anne Marie's leadership and do exactly as she says, but not because of her vision or charisma. One has moved dozens of times before, and knows this is a five-block drive over residential streets with no bumps, so how well the truck is loaded is not critical. The other doesn't care who loads the truck, how, or how well. He is just happy to not have that job for the tenth time.

Anne Marie's one act of leadership, her twenty-second effort to initiate *intentional influence*, encounters numerous endorsement-related responses, one or more for each person she is attempting to lead. Some of these will be palpable, some undetectable, some verbal, some silent. Further, how her leadership is endorsed has as much to do with others' goals as it does with her power. Finally, this endorsement process may go on long after the move is over. Some may approach Anne Marie later to help them move. Others may consciously avoid inviting her.

Ongoing Leadership

The above example is illustrative but limited. The group is made up of volunteers, and the purpose is a specific, immediate task.

Leadership settings are usually ongoing, with more complex task and relationship goals. How might the endorsement process change if the setting changed, and would endorsement still be a factor? Suppose Anne Marie is the manager of an inbound call center team helping callers with software problems for a fee. Everyone on the team is paid, and Anne Marie has been in her position for two years. This is now a professional setting with formally established leadership. Are the forms of power at work no longer subject to endorsement, negotiated endorsement, or partial endorsement? Is resistance no longer a factor? In short, will Anne Marie's leadership now produce exactly the outcome goals and relationship goals she intends? Does she no longer need to concern herself with what kind of leader she is?

Endorsement and Trust—a First Look

Endorsement is perhaps most tangibly demonstrated in the simple, implicit yet explicit relational act of trusting, such as when people do start bringing Anne Marie boxes. Consider how many people a person voluntarily endorses when she takes the trusting step of boarding an airplane, driving down a two-lane road, or buying a can of food. In all of these examples, one person endorses with her very well-being that a chain of people she will never meet have power and that the whole interconnected chain is trustworthy.

Endorsement is Instinctive

Just like power is a subtle factor in every interpersonal interaction, so is the endorsement of power. Folger, Poole, and Stutman describe how "the tendency to endorse power is deep-seated and based in powerful and pervasive social processes. At the most superficial level, we endorse power because the resources it is based on enable others to grant or deny things that are valuable."[7] One person may endorse another as a conscious, careful decision, or

---

7. Ibid., 141.

based solely on appearances. "We endorse those we expect to be powerful and do not endorse those we expect to be weak."[8] Endorsement is often an instinctive process, based on unconscious assumptions, as is the decision to deny endorsement. Prejudice and distrust play strong roles in the endorsement process. "The tendency and willingness to endorse power stems from several sources, including preconceptions about what makes a person weak or strong, an aura of mystery, a the judicial use of authority, and evidence of valued skills or abilities."[9]

The Ironic Power of Endorsement

Still, much effort to exert influence can be met with a simple act of non-endorsement. The offer of a thirty-day free trial and free shipping may not persuade the TV buyer. Senator Talbert may use several tactics in a months-long effort to secure a fellow legislator's "Yae" vote on an upcoming bill, only to see her vote "Nay." This illustrates another key aspect of endorsement. Senator Talbert values his colleague's vote, so she can continue to influence *his* behavior for months simply by not making a decision. Refusing the other incentives may bring the TV salesperson to drop the price. In short, the endorsement of power is itself a source of power, in that it can be influence another's actions. These possibilities, and the fact that endorsement determines if someone else has power, contribute to **the irony of endorsement**: the endorsement of power can be more powerful than power.

Misinterpreting Endorsement

The examples of endorsement used up to this point have been active and conscious such as retrieving heavy boxes for Anne Marie or a soldier following orders. But endorsement can be passive and silent, such as listening or not disagreeing. *Qui tacit consentire.*

8. Ibid., 143.
9. Ibid., 141.

One challenge with such forms of *passive endorsement* is that they can easily be misinterpreted. A student listening to a professor in a lecture hall, for example, may be a sign that she understands what he is saying, or that she does not understand but is embarrassed to show it, or that she is disengaged and day-dreaming. The professor may not know whether learning has taken place until the final exam—too late to achieve his purposes. This and any other example of delayed endorsement corresponds with the systems theory concept of *feedback delay*.[10]

ENDORSEMENT OF LEADERSHIP

That every act of leadership is by definition an act of social power, along with the studied reality that social power must be endorsed, alludes to *the first irony of leader endorsement*: the endorsement by those led ultimately defines leadership more than the leader. Consider that every definition of leadership presented in chapter 2 is also a compelling call to gain some specific form of endorsement. Hesburgh's definition of leadership, for example, is subtly but equally a prescription for how to attain endorsement: "The very essence of leadership is that you have to have vision. It's got to be a vision you articulate clearly and forcefully on every occasion. You can't blow an uncertain trumpet." Because if you do, your leadership won't be endorsed.

Leaders navigate endorsement constantly as they lead, and it drives many familiar questions leaders ask, such as:

- How do we get people to catch the vision?
- How do I get buy-in on this change?
- How can we motivate the students to take ownership?
- How do we get the employees on board?

If power was the property of the individual leader, and endorsement was not a consideration, questions like these would not

---

10. Senge, *Fifth Discipline*, 80.

exist. Leadership would be just as every leader intended. Leaders would be a commodity. Context would not matter, every purpose would be achieved, and leadership would not be an engaging, artistic challenge. Two leaders with the same goals in the same situation would achieve the same results. And every leader in history, including those too terrible to list, would have succeeded.

Instead questions like these, and the reality of endorsement implicit within them, define leadership settings. Leaders lead by how they navigate the endorsement process. And ultimately, those led do as much or more to define leadership settings as leaders do.

ENDORSEMENT BY LEADERSHIP

Endorsement can be proactive, prompting some act of power. For example, a VP may entrust a regional manager with new responsibilities, or simply ask for advice, or encourage her by saying, "You can do it." These examples reiterate how endorsing someone else's power is actually an act of power in itself, a means to bring about desired outcomes.

In fact, many definitions of leadership, especially those that emphasize the connection between outcome and relationship, challenge the leader to prioritize endorsing those she leads:

> Before you are a leader, success is all about growing yourself. When you become a leader, success is all about growing others.[11]
>
> —*Jack Welch*

> Outstanding leaders go out of their way to boost the self-esteem of their personnel. If people believe in themselves, it's amazing what they can accomplish.[12]
>
> —*Sam Walton*

---

11. Kruse, "100 Best Quotes on Leadership."
12. Ibid.

As we look ahead into the next century, leaders will be those who empower others.[13]

—Bill Gates

These insights and examples illustrate **the second irony of leader endorsement**: the leader gains far more power by effectively endorsing the power of those he leads than he does by them endorsing his power.

Endorsement is empowerment at its most basic, authentic level. Put in stark but necessary terms, empowerment *without* endorsement is at the least ineffective, and quite possibly inauthentic. Like leaders, those led need power, and so need endorsement. "Without some exercise of power in your interpersonal relationships, you would soon feel worthless as a person."[14] Hence anyone who leads, or wants to, would do well to ask herself the basic question: *What do I do to empower those I lead by authentically and relationally endorsing them?*

LISTENING AS LEADERSHIP

Robert Greenleaf succinctly connects endorsement, listening, and empowerment when observing the transformations in people trained to listen: "It is because true listening builds strength in other people."[15] Peter Block also connects transformation, power and leadership with listening:

> Listening may be the single most powerful action the leader can take. Leaders will always be under pressure to speak, but if building social fabric is important, and sustained transformation is the goal, then listening becomes the greater service.[16]

---

13. Ibid.
14. Hocker and Wilmot, *Interpersonal Conflict*, 116.
15. Greenleaf, *Power of Servant Leadership*, 31.
16. Block, *Community*, 88.

Echoing this refrain, Jim Collins, author of *Built to Last* and *Good to Great*, describes sobering but empowering advice he heard from an elder:

> During my first year on the Stanford faculty in 1988, I sought out professor John Gardner for guidance on how I might become a better teacher. Gardner, former Secretary of Health, Education and Welfare, founder of Common Cause, and author of the classic text *Self-Renewal*, stung me with a comment that changed my life. "It occurs to me, Jim, that you spend too much time trying to be interesting," he said. "Why don't you invest more time being interested?"[17]

A leader listening is a potentially vulnerable and inefficient process, yet a profound opportunity for the leader and the led to mutually endorse one another. And that leadership setting in which such mutual endorsement takes place may be, by any definition, the most powerful imaginable. However, beyond potential vulnerability and inefficiency, chapter 13 lists several other familiar reasons why leaders might resist endorsing those they lead.

Given the respected observations by Greenleaf, Block and Collins, several candid, practical questions arise for leaders in any setting: *How much time and effort do I expend listening to those I lead? How does this compare to the amount of time I expect them to listen to me? Do I listen well? Do I listen as well as I want to be listened to?*

THE VIOLENT EXCEPTION

A person's social power is determined through endorsement, with one troubling yet ubiquitous exception: "Excluding situations of unequal physical power and use of violence, power is a property of the social relationship rather than a quality of the individual."[18]

---

17. Collins, "Why Business Thinking Is Not the Answer," author's note.
18. Hocker and Wilmot, *Interpersonal Conflict*, 116.

Physical force, including violence, is the one form of social power that an individual can *have*, and force upon others, without their endorsement. Violence, be it a fist to the face, a gun aimed at a leader, or a leader calling for a fire hose to be aimed at a crowd, is an inherently coercive and competing form of power available to anyone able to use it, including the person who *resorts to violence* when other forms of power are not endorsed. In fact, one appeal of violent power is that it simplifies relationships by casting the endorsement process aside—"Do as I say or I'll shoot." Violent power, including the many ironies that often accompany it, is examined in detail in chapter 12.

Still, violence is no guarantee of power. One party may injure or even kill another and still not achieve the purposes intended. And in some cases the use of violence not only thwarts the purposes of the violent but also furthers the purposes of the victim. Call this **the martyr's irony** or *the irony of Martin Luther King Jr.*, as it lies at the heart of non-violent resistance.

> ## Endorsement in The Church
>
> Jesus Christ is wholly familiar with the endorsement process:
>
>> From this time many of his disciples turned back and no longer followed him. (John 6:66)
>>
>> These people honor me with their lips, but their hearts are far from me. (Matt 15:8)
>>
>> [Thomas] said to them, "Unless I see the nail marks in his hands and put my finger where the nails were, and put my hand into his side, I will not believe." (John 20:25b)
>
> And consider the endorsement of God's power inherent in:
>
> | | | | | |
> |---|---|---|---|---|
> | faith | hope | thanksgiving | worship | confession |
> | repentance | obedience | intercession | peace | joy |
> | service | evangelism | following | praise | tithing |
>
> While each of these is much more than endorsement, all are agreements that God has power. All help bring about God's desired outcomes, and all *are* God's desired outcomes. In short, The Church exists to endorse the Power of God. Further, these help make sense of the fact that the endorsement of power can itself be a form of power. E.g. Prayer is powerful in that it endorses God's power, and calls that power into circumstances.
>
> And, while love is often described as a form of power—i.e. *the power of love*—love must be appreciated as endorsement too. To see this, note the similarity in the following two statements. One is a definition and one an example. Note how both describe purposive influence, and both describe endorsement of that influence.
>
>> Kipnis: Power is said to be exercised when changes occur in the target person's behavior that can be attributed to the powerholder's influence and that serve the powerholder's interests and intentions. Furthermore, these changes would ordinarily not have been carried out by the target person.[19]
>>
>> John: We love because he first loved us. (1 John 4:19)
>
> 19. Kipnis, *Powerholders*, 82.

How Often I Have Longed . . .

> O Jerusalem, Jerusalem, you who kill the prophets and stone those I sent to you, how often I have longed to gather your children together, as a hen gathers her chicks under her wings, but you were not willing. (Matthew 23:35)

God subjects his Power to the process of endorsement. The familiar term for this is *free will*. One early example of this involves two people and a disobedient reach for a piece of fruit (see Genesis 3). "The sin of the garden was the sin of power."[20] They wanted to be like God. This was also a sin of disobedience, of withdrawing endorsement.

The Creator has always allowed the created to reject him, even as he fervidly details the consequences. The tree of the knowledge of good and evil served as a constant herald to consciously trust God by refraining from disobedience; to voluntarily endorse God through restraint. What other means did they have to experience active faith, to consciously choose God? Another question may as well be asked: Was the knowledge of good and evil within the fruit itself, or within the disobedient, power hungry reach for it?

Jesus crafts many parables in which the God figure is lightly spurned by those beneath him. In his parable of the prodigal son (see Luke 15), Jesus describes the father in almost piteous terms: in how he just hands over his wealth, in how he runs to his wayward son upon returning, and in how he turns the other cheek when his older son berates him. Jesus himself laments his own powerlessness, using lowly images like a shepherd and a brooding hen to describe himself.

God's divine Power, however immense, is individual, not social power. Creation was accomplished through divine Power: God was alone. But what God seeks from us must come through relationship. Those expecting or preferring a majestic, overpowering God should not be surprised to encounter instead someone willing to cast Power aside, and someone willing to be cast aside.

---

20. Foster, *Challenge of the Disciplined Life*, 175.

> ### "You are blessed, Simon…"
>
> > "But what about you?" Jesus asked. "Who do you say that I am?" Simon Peter answered, "You are the Christ, the Son of the living God." And Jesus answered him, "You are blessed, Simon son of Jonah, because flesh and blood did not reveal this to you, but my Father in heaven! And I tell you that you are Peter, and on this rock I will build my church, and the gates of Hades will not overcome it."
> > (Matthew 16:15–18)
>
> Jesus asks and listens, and Peter endorses Jesus as God. Then Jesus, in overwhelming, joyful detail, endorses the Power of God at work in Peter. Several telling questions involving both Power and power arise. First, would Peter have known such Power was at work in him without Jesus' endorsement? How else would he know this was even possible? How else would the others know?
>
> Second, is Jesus leading here? Does Jesus seek to intentionally influence his disciples by listening, discerning, and joyfully proclaiming Power working in someone else? Third, is Peter's faith that Jesus is God really that Powerful? Is this basic appreciation the necessary sediment that Jesus will use to build up Peter as his rock? It better be, because under his own power Peter is better known for failures than his successes.
>
> Finally, did this leadership setting just happen? Or is Jesus deliberately modeling how to lead by listening, and by endorsing what God is doing through others? Regardless, he is certainly demonstrating the joy that comes from this kind of leadership.

...in Order to Wait on Tables

> In those days when the number of disciples was increasing, the Grecian Jews among them complained against the Hebraic Jews because their widows were being overlooked in the daily distribution of food. So the Twelve gathered all the disciples together and said, "It would not be right for us to neglect the ministry of the word of God in order to wait on tables. Brothers, choose seven men among you who are known to be full of the Spirit and wisdom. We will turn this responsibility over to them." This proposal pleased the whole group. They chose Stephen, a man full of the Holy Spirit; also Philip, Procurus, Nicanor, Timon, Parmenas, and Nicolas from Antioch, a convert to Judaism. They presented these men the apostles, who prayed and laid their hands on them. (Acts 6:1–6)

This is a good example of needs analysis, collaborative problem solving, endorsement by leadership, and empowerment. And were it not for the Power of the Spirit, it would end there. But instead, Luke must record the rest of Acts 6, along with Acts 7 and 8.

First, Stephen, described as "a man full of God's grace and power," (6:8) goes and gets himself killed. But only after delivering arguably the best sermon in all of Scripture, considering the extemporaneous setting, exhaustive detail, thorough exegesis, clarity of message, and ultimately tough crowd.

Meanwhile Philip takes off: first to Samaria, where his preaching and miracles compel Peter and John to catch up to him (Acts 8:14), not to bring him back, but to endorse what the Spirit is doing through him. Then, as they return to Jerusalem, Philip continues on. On their 42 mile walk back to Jerusalem, Peter and John may have pondered the irony that they had empowered Philip in order to make their lives easier.

Peter and John face a challenge unique to church leadership: preparing and raising up others to meet known ministry needs, and then flexibly and retrospectively endorsing what else the Spirit wants to do through them. Further, Stephen and Philip model how gifted obedience may look like being willing to wait tables.

> ## Should We Talk about Endorsement in Church?
>
> Questions confronting other leaders confront church leaders too. How do I get the congregation to catch the vision? How do I get buy-in from older members? In fact, church leaders today are deluged with the most daunting of endorsement-related questions:
>
>> What if we could know with confidence that the steps we're asking people to take will actually move them closer to Christ?[21]
>>
>> Can we find some way to prevent discussion about worship styles from becoming fierce and bitter battles waged between two entrenched camps?[22]
>>
>> Where did we get the idea that spiritual maturity can be achieved apart from an integration of the emotional aspects of who we are?[23]
>>
>> If Christian community is not available or not being pursued, what can we really hope to accomplish together and as individuals who really do long to belong?[24]
>>
>> In other words, plenty of people in this country are interested in spiritual matters. They are simply not going to church to feed this interest. Why?[25]
>>
>> How do I get younger people to come, stay, and become active participants in ministry[?][26]
>
> These questions are among the weightiest any leader could ponder. All could be, and likely are, prayers. All involve both power and Power, and all illustrate the process of endorsement.
>
> ---
>
> 21. Hawkins and Parkinson, *Follow Me*, 5.
> 22. Dawn, *Reaching Out without Dumbing Down*, 3.
> 23. Scazzero, *Emotionally Healthy Church*, 53.
> 24. Frazee, *Connecting Church*, 241.
> 25. Duin, *Quitting Church*, 13.
> 26. Menconi, *Intergenerational Church*, 12

Endorsement

> Take this cup from me ...
>
>> And the Lord God commanded the man, "You are free to eat from any tree in the garden; but you must not eat from the tree of the knowledge of good and evil, for when you eat of it you will surely die." (Genesis 2:16–17)
>>
>> When the woman saw that the fruit of the tree was good for food and pleasing to the eye, and also desirable for gaining wisdom, she took some and ate it. She also gave some to her husband, and he ate it. (Genesis 3:6)
>>
>> Father if you are willing, take this cup from me; yet not my will, but yours be done. (Luke 22:41)
>
> The Christian view of reality finds itself framed between two gardens. Two curiously contrasting choices, made in these two curiously comparable settings, form how Christians assess the world around them.
>
> In the first garden, endorsement of God's will is withdrawn, almost casually. In the second, God's will is endorsed despite mortal anguish. The first involves a woman and man reaching for vast power and identity; reaching to make themselves like God, knowing good and evil. The second involves a man giving up all power; a man, "[w]ho, being in very nature God, did not consider equality with God something to be grasped, but made himself nothing." (Philippians 2:6). This second man, good by all accounts, chooses to know evil to its very fullest extent.
>
> The disobedient decision in the first garden necessitates the obedient decision in the second. Both choices lead to death, and death clearly promised beforehand, as a consequence of sin. Most curiously, the first decision involves the disobedient taking of forbidden whole fruit, and the second an obedient, metaphorical acceptance of unwanted crushed fruit.
>
> Is there irony somewhere in this? If so, call it **the irony of two gardens**. Another question: is this happenstance situational irony, or intended dramatic irony?

CHAPTER 7

Other People's Power: Six Orientations

> If you compare yourself with others, you may become vain and bitter; for always there will be greater and lesser persons than yourself.
>
> —MAX ERMANN, DESIDARATA

> It is necessary for me to establish a winner image. Therefore, I have to beat somebody.
>
> —RICHARD M. NIXON

Leadership settings may perform according to desired outcomes, but they behave according to how people feel about other people's power. Is this a *collaborative* or *CYA* culture; a *learning* or *top-down* environment? Is the boss a mentor, or did he assemble a team of rivals?

As introduced in chapter 5, one person may un-or semi-consciously assess another person's power from at least 6 instinctive orientations: comparing, competing, expansive, collaborating, designated, and sufficient/insufficient.

Before exploring these orientations further, several factors merit note. First, a person can experience more than one of these orientations at the same time, even within the same relationship. For example, two people may collaborate around task goals but pursue different, effectively competing relationship goals. Second, these orientations may be retrospective or prospective. One person may adopt a competing orientation based on perceptions during a relationship, or bring a competitive disposition with her into the relationship. Third, these orientations can be self-fulfilling. For example, if one person relates to another in a condescending way, reflecting an insufficient orientation, the other may perceive himself as insufficient. Fourth, these orientations determine a one person's willingness to endorse another person's power. If I have a collaborating orientation toward your power, I may look for ways to endorse you. But if I have a competing orientation toward you, I will be inclined to resist your power for my own. Fifth, any orientation may define a fleeting relationship, such as when two pedestrians lunge toward the last seat on the train. Or they may define an ongoing relationship, such as a professor emeritus expansively mentoring a doctoral student toward her dissertation. Finally, a leader can have any and all of these orientations toward individuals he seeks to lead, and vice versa.

A COMPARING ORIENTATION

This orientation, which could also be called *sociometric*, is heard in terms like *upper middle class, high end,* and *getting ahead.* I assess my power by using others' power as a standard. This orientation fuels jealousy and envy, but it can also be inspiring, such as when a ten-year-old uses chooses a role model, saying, "Someday I am going to be like her." Other familiar phrases like "Moving up in the world" and "Keeping up with the Jones's" illustrate the motivational aspect of comparing.

Any adjective on a person's resume—*fast learner, seasoned, natural, expert*—reflects how she compares her power to others: resumes themselves are vehicles to enable comparison, as are standardized tests. Leadership settings are saturated with comparisons: *upper management, entry level, top-down, bottom-up, in the trenches.*

A COMPETING ORIENTATION

This is a comparing orientation as well, but with a perception that "power is fixed and finite and that there is only so much power to go around."[1] This orientation, also called "power over,"[2] "dominant,"[3] and "either/or,"[4] perceives that one party gains power by taking it from others. Settings with finite outcomes, such as three internal candidates vying for the same open position, or mine-worker teams seeking a fewest accidents bonus, foster this orientation. Strong and close is the connection between competition and high performance.

This orientation can be absorbing, in part because it determines a winner. Stadiums are built to observe competition. This orientation beckons me whenever I believe your power can threaten my purposes and concerns. "The implicit assumption in this type of conceptualization of power is that power relations are inherently coercive and competitive; the more power A has, the less power available to B."[5] While a competing orientation views high power and power imbalance as ideal, chapter 13 will address several ironies that qualify this assumption.

The Chronic Competitor

The person with a *competitive disposition*, or what Coleman calls a "chronic competitive approach to power,"[6] tends to bring a win/lose perspective into any setting. A conversation about the weather can become a contest. If you are right then I must be wrong, and if you are wrong then I must be right. A penchant for *one-upmanship, fault-finding,* and always *needing to get the last word in* are symptoms of a competitive disposition. How common is it for me to feel jealous, envious, or just cold toward other the accomplish-

---

1. Coleman and Deutsch, *Handbook of Conflict Resolution*, 110.
2. Ibid.
3. Hocker and Wilmot, *Interpersonal Conflict*, 108.
4. Ibid.
5. Coleman et al., *Handbook of Conflict Resolution*, 112.
6. Ibid. 122.

ments of others? How resistant am I to endorsing another person's power? When the queen in *Snow White*, for example, keeps asking the mirror, "Who is the fairest one of all?" she is modeling a competitive disposition toward all other people.

This competitive disposition demonstrated by the queen merits close scrutiny for at least two reasons. First, the queen brings a win/lose orientation to a subjective and intangible concern. Greatness, reality, morality, or the best flavor of ice cream—all can be argued from a competing orientation. Winning such an argument, however, demonstrates only the confidence to believe I did win. Subjective assessments remain subjective. The ethereal remains unchanged. Many questions are simply not answered by who wins and who loses, or how the majority of people vote.

Second, the queen's competitive question caters specifically to her identity. She is not competing according to her ability to achieve a purpose (task goals) or her ability to influence others (relational goals). Instead she openly asks an identity-serving question often silently asked within groups: "Who among us is the greatest?" This question, in whatever form it takes, will redefine any leadership setting in which it is asked, be it a boardroom, a playground, the sideline of a youth soccer game, or a supper table.

A COLLABORATING ORIENTATION

This orientation, also called "power with,"[7] "both/and,"[8] and "mutual,"[9] perceives that all parties' power can increase simultaneously, or at least that one party's increasing power does not automatically mean another's decreases. Examples of a collaborating orientation vary greatly, depending on the goals parties bring to the relationship. One person slowing down to let another change lanes is one example, and quality circles are another. But so is a

---

7. Coleman et al., *Handbook of Conflict Resolution*, 113.
8. Hocker and Wilmot, *Interpersonal Conflict*, 108.
9. Ibid. 110.

mom maintaining her "best mom ever" status by buying vodka for her fourteen-year-old son and his friends.

Any form of teamwork demands a collaborating orientation, precisely because the same team often encounters competing interests, both internally and externally. In fact, collaborating often looks like cooperative competing. The familiar question, "What are some ways we can balance the budget?" demonstrates this. "Making the project work, moving toward mutual goals, and getting a new effort up and running require skills very different from those used with either/or power."[10] Nevertheless, scholars describe that while a collaborating orientation is the natural orientation in some cultures, and "often the first choice of women in our culture," a competitive orientation is more common to men and to U.S. culture in general.[11]

AN EXPANSIVE ORIENTATION

An *expansive orientation*, also called "power to,"[12] regards another person's increasing power not merely as fine or good, but as success. The expansive orientation seeks to make others "empowered and independent."[13] For example, expanding and endorsing the power of his children is perhaps the central responsibility of a parent, knowing that someday his children will need to *make it on their own*. This orientation also is seen in familiar roles such as teacher, coach, and mentor. An expansive leader may hear that daring, innovative call to *empowerment* and quietly say, "Um . . . duh." Consider the plain connection these thought leaders make between expansive leadership, endorsement, and empowerment:

> The final test of a leader is that he leaves behind him in other men the conviction and the will to carry on.
>
> —*Walter Lippmann*

10. Ibid. 109.
11. Ibid. 110.
12. Coleman et al., *Handbook of Conflict Resolution*, 110.
13. Ibid.

Other People's Power: Six Orientations

> Leadership is unlocking people's potential to become better.
>
> —Bill Bradley

> Management is about arranging and telling. Leadership is about nurturing and enhancing.
>
> —Tom Peters

Such inspiring admonishments are well and good, but they merit at least two cautions. First, the expansive leader is the most dangerous of all—to herself, to those she leads, and to others. A leader with this orientation exposes everyone in the vicinity to greater and greater risk. As the flight instructor's pupil learns to fly, she will risk crashing them both many times. And she will risk harming herself and others every time she flies afterwards. Second, expansive leaders traffic in failure. The expect it, plan for it, dwell on it, work to learn from it, and ideally instill a healthy attitude toward it. Indeed, without the potential for failure, the expansive leader would be unnecessary

In this way, an expansive orientation rigorously results in the most power and the most risk for everyone involved. The flight instructor succeeds when someone else can fly, navigating all the dangers associated. The parent succeeds when the child can cross the street alone.

In fact, within those expansive leadership settings where power is being poured out—during the game, during the first solo flight, during the final exam, during the mission—the expansive leader may be *on the sidelines, on the ground, back at base*, effectively powerless and dependent. Call this **the mentor's irony**.

An expansive leader knows he has succeeded when the ones he leads are *able to bring about desired outcomes* without him around. This leader may find the most joy in saying, "You will do greater things than I have." The parent with the expansive orientation rejoices, perhaps through bittersweet tears, when his child can walk *away*, ride her bicycle *away*, swim *away*, drive *away*, and move *away*.

A DESIGNATED ORIENTATION

We have a *designated orientation* toward elected officials, teachers, law enforcement, judges, employers, and anyone else we formally give power to. Designated power is legitimate power formally, and often ceremoniously, given to another. But the residents of a state designate power to a governor to achieve our own goals. Hence that governor serves while in office. Consider another example: by giving authority to a football referee, players defer to that referee and suspend their impulse to *take matters into their own hands*. That referee in turn benefits the teams and their fans by creating a fair setting for the teams to determine which is best.

This book will discuss designated power further by equating it with given authority. Chapter 11 takes a longer look at given authority, including contrasting it with other forms of authority, and describing the four directions from which authority can be given.

A SUFFICIENT/INSUFFICIENT ORIENTATION

The previous orientations have a relational focus: How does your power compare to mine? In contrast, a **sufficient orientation** toward other people's power focuses on outcomes. Do I instinctively believe you are able to *achieve purposes* I value? Does a basketball point guard shoot first or pass the ball, trusting his teammates to score? An **insufficient orientation** assumes another person is not able to achieve a valued purpose. One example is a *helicopter parent* who hovers around his child, not trusting her to face her challenges on her own, or the new mother who assumes her husband cannot soothe their crying baby, and tries to take it from him. I may conclude you have insufficient power based on your age, gender, level of education, skin color, or nationality. This orientation is behind the sentiment that *if you want something done right you have to do it yourself.* Examples of an insufficient orientation in leadership settings include a program director micromanaging or *snoopervising* employees, a business owner who cannot take a vacation because he is sure operations will fall apart in his absence, and a group of shareholders who believe a CEO candidate is unqualified because she's a she.

An involved example of an insufficient orientation within a leader comes in the fifth book of the Harry Potter series, during which the main character spends much of the school year training his schoolmates to use magic in self-defense. He observes their success, compliments them as they demonstrate capability rivaling his own, and even voices his pride in their skills. Yet when faced with actually depending on them he reflexively, even incredulously resists, assuming only he is able to face the book's climactic danger.[14]

These examples point to an insufficient orientation as an instinctive, unconscious lack of trust. "We endorse those we expect to be powerful and do not endorse those we expect to be weak."[15] However, an insufficient orientation can be intentional; a means of control. Fiske describes, for example, how high power enables stereotyping, and how stereotyping can be a means to maintain a preferred power imbalance.[16]

COMPETING OR COLLABORATING OR EXPANSIVE?

Where does the greatest contrast lie? Does the competing orientation differ most from the collaborating orientation? Does the expansive orientation, which exists to increase power, contrast most the competing orientation, which sees power as a finite sum to be taken or lost? A more revealing question to ask is: how do these orientations coexist?

Can competition exist within a collaborative environment, such as when a work team votes on how to proceed with a project? Can an expansive leader resort to a competitive setting, such as when a football coach has the offense and defense scrimmage each other?

14. Rowling, *Harry Potter and the Order of the Phoenix*, 761.
15. Folger et al., *Working Through Conflict*, 143.
16. Fiske, "Controlling Other People," 623.

In short, should a leader work to foster a collaborative or expansive or competitive environment, or should that leader instead employ these orientations as needed, recognizing that each helps the group to accomplish its purposes?

EXPANSIVE AND INSUFFICIENT

At first glance, an insufficient orientation toward another's power may seem contradictory or even the opposite of an expansive orientation. But the two are complementary, even symbiotic. A baseball coach with an expansive orientation expects, perhaps even enjoys, a bunch of kids who begin with an insufficient ability to play the game. A math teacher would be in a bad position if her incoming students already knew the material she plans to teach them. An expansive leader expects to escort those she leads from insufficient to sufficient power.

And the expansive leader fosters settings in which this transformation can be assessed. The math teacher gives an exam over the material presented, and then covers this material again on the final. The coach divides up his own team for a scrimmage in preparation for their next game.

THE LECTURE HALL IRONY

The previous chapter used the example of a student silently listening in a professor's class, possibly because she understands, or because she is daydreaming, or because she is lost but embarrassed to admit it. The same relational action, passive listening, may indicate endorsement or non-endorsement. The student may even disagree, but not attempt to interrupt because she fears getting on the professor's *bad side*. This indicates endorsement of the professor's legitimate power and imposing relational nature, but non-endorsement of his expertise. Meanwhile, the professor does not know if his desired outcome, learning, is taking place or not. He is a designated leader, but is he *intentionally influencing* or *bringing about desired outcomes*? Does he have expert power, or merely authority? He may not know if he has achieved his desired outcomes until he grades the final—too late to empower and too late to achieve his purposes. Call this **the lecture hall irony**. It is brought about when the leader controls many forms of power and all are endorsed passively.

The expansive professor may address this irony by simply incorporating dialog into his lecture. This allows and even forces students to reveal their understanding, or disagreement, or confusion. With the simple step of asking and listening, the professor changes passive endorsement to an active negotiation of his power. And this negotiation will do much to confirm if he is successful at transferring knowledge. He will know immediately if he is achieving his purposes or not. In short, by asking and listening, the professor goes far beyond mere professing. He has reduced the feedback delay to the point where the whole setting can benefit from it and make adjustments. Further, he may actually be able to endorse, encourage, and foster ownership. Students will also be much less inclined to day-dream in class.

EXPANSIVE CORRECTION

For an example of how these six orientations can combine within the same leadership setting, consider the following interaction:

> Three starting members of high school soccer team show up 15 minutes late for practice. The coach listens to their explanation, nods and calmly responds, "Tell 'em." The three, with some anger, shame and tears, inform the rest of the team that, per the team covenant, they are benched for the next match.

In many ways, this interaction exemplifies a competitive orientation. The coach takes a power over stance toward the players, relies on coercive power of punishment, and the outcome is zero-sum. The coach wins the argument, and the players lose. But the entire interaction demonstrates the players' respect for the designated power of both the coach and the covenant. And making the covenant requires collaborating, as does abiding by it. Also, the coach fostered adoption of the team covenant before the season began, an act of ecological power, possibly inspired by her experience. She's developed a healthy insufficient orientation toward her players *ability to bring about desired outcomes*. She knew this day might come.

But ultimately, this interaction is expansive. All aspects of it, including everything that lead up to it, unfolded because this leader prioritizes the learning and growth of her players beyond winning. The increased sense of responsibility, the tangible awareness that individual actions can have consequences to the group, and that growth often comes at the expense of one's identity, are among the many lessons the entire team, not just the three tardy players, will learn from this episode.

Further, this example also demonstrates the connection between expansive leadership and the six orientations toward other peoples' power. Expansive leaders—teachers, coaches, mentors—constantly juggle, leverage and combine these orientations more than any other kind of leader.

HOW ORIENTATIONS COMBINE

Our orientations toward other people's power constantly impact leadership settings. Consider several reasonable combinations as examples:

- A leader has an expansive orientation toward those he leads, while they have a competing orientation toward each other.
- A leader has a collaborating orientation toward some she leads, because she likes them, and a competing orientation toward others she dislikes.
- A team has a collaborating orientation toward the main goal, but individuals have a competing orientation concerning the specific means to achieve that goal.

- A leader has a sufficient orientation toward some she leads and assumes an insufficient orientation toward others, based on assumptions around such things as gender, education, and nationality.
- A workplace bully is highly depended upon, and hence collaborated with, to achieve group task goals, despite him competing around face and identity goals, demeaning others to elevate himself.
- A group has an ongoing collaborative relationship that carefully incorporates competitive episodes, such as when a nonprofit committee considers how to spend grant funds.
- A critical mass (literally) of those led have a collaborating orientation toward one another and share a competing orientation toward the leader.

These examples and myriad others help to illustrate how orientations constantly impact, define, and redefine leadership settings.

> ## Welcome to The Church
>
> Anyone arguing that men can possibly, sometimes, maybe have a competitive disposition need look no further than Jesus' disciples, who maintained a running "Who is the greatest?" argument (see Luke 9 and 22) right up through Jesus' betrayal, and beyond.
>
> And it wasn't just the men. The mother of James and John shows an opportunistic competitive streak. When Jesus foretells that he will be "mocked and flogged and crucified," her immediate and clearly faithful response is not grief or dismay. Instead she leverages the circumstances, albeit reverently, coming to kneel before Jesus and request reserved seats for her sons beside him in heaven (Matthew 20:19–21). This bold and competitive move may be the reason Jesus dubs her boys the "Sons of Thunder" (Mark 3:17).
>
> Where did Jesus come up with these people? And why? It's as if he seeks out the most envious, petty individuals he can find, and patiently transforms them into leaders.
>
> Nothing has changed. These first leaders serve Jesus' purposes by modeling the temptations that await those that follow. Even C.S. Lewis, among the most respected of church leaders, reflecting on Jesus work in him, confessed:
>
>> All my acts, desires, and thoughts were to be brought into harmony with universal Spirit. For the first time I examined myself with a seriously practical purpose. And there I found what appalled me; a zoo of lusts, a bedlam of ambitions, a nursery of fears, a harem of fondled hatreds. My name was legion.[17]
>
> Church leaders should not be surprised by same vulnerable challenge faced by the disciples and Lewis. They may be called to lead by confession, facing their instinctive temptations to compare and compete, while inviting those they lead into their own very human transformation.
>
> ---
>
> 17. Lewis, *Surprised by Joy*, 226.

But you are not to be like that

> [Also] a dispute arose among them as to which of them was considered to be the greatest. Jesus said to them, "The kings of the Gentiles lord it over them, and those who exercise authority over them call themselves 'Benefactors.' But you are not to be like that. Instead; the greatest among you must become like the youngest, and the one who rules like the one who serves." (Luke 22:24–25)

Jesus sternly but expansively corrects his leaders-in-training, commanding them to forsake their competitive dispositions, while naming how benevolent titles can provide a thin disguise. Jesus frequently points out good examples of bad leadership because he knows the temptations that await his own. All his examples involve the competitive, self-expanding approach to power.

Consider also Jesus' and Peter's mutual rebuke in Matthew 16. Jesus has just stated that he must go to Jerusalem, and be killed and raised to life. Peter, understandably, cannot fathom this most anti-competitive spiritual reality: for Jesus and those around him to gain everything he offers, everything must be taken from him.

> Peter took him aside and began to rebuke him: "Never Lord! This shall never happen to you!" But he turned and said to Peter, "Get behind me, Satan! You are a stumbling block to me; you do not have in mind the things of God, but the things of men." (Matt 16:22–23)

In both these passages Jesus leads through intimate expansive correction. Still, were these scathing rebukes appropriate? Did they strengthen or weaken the disciples? Did he respect Peter's dignity? But most importantly, how did Jesus form the candid, familiar relationships these passages portray? How did he forge such durable community, so that this close, frank correction was not only possible, but inspiring?

CHAPTER 8

Dependence

> You only have power over people so long as you don't take everything away from them. But when you've robbed a man of everything, he's no longer in your power he's free again.
>
> —ALEXANDER SOLZHENITSYN

Dependence mirrors power. One person's power, as chapter 2 introduced, is determined by another person's dependence. "Power is based on one person's dependence on resources or currencies that another person controls, or seems to possess."[1] My power decreases as you depend on me less. As leader or led, your power increases as I depend on you more. And, as any elite team in any setting recognizes, our mutual power increases exponentially as we depend on each other more.

VOLUNTARY AND INVOLUNTARY DEPENDENCE

My power over you may have much to do with how difficult it is for you to reduce or end that dependence. A cable provider, for example, may raise its rates knowing that its customers will pay

---

1. Hocker and Wilmot, *Interpersonal Conflict*, 116.

the higher fees rather than go through the difficulty of finding a new provider. The power of a monopoly can be described as *involuntary dependence*. You must depend upon me even though you do not trust me, or even distrust me. Ebenezer Scrooge had Bob Cratchett working late on Christmas Eve, for next to nothing, primarily because Cratchett desperately needed the job. The absolute power Lord Acton described as absolutely corrupting requires absolute involuntary dependence. Any bullying situation requires that the bully be involuntarily depended upon somehow. An office bully, for example, likely has some special skill the company cannot replace easily. This factor helps define the dilemma faced by the bullied, and those observing it.

Trust, in contrast, is **voluntary dependence**. Trust is the choice to depend on someone else's power, such as when a passenger boards an airplane. In this way, trust is perhaps the most common and authentic form of endorsement. If I trust you, any power you have, even that approaching absolute power, can never be absolute, because your power is still a factor of my endorsement. My dependence, and along with it your power, can increase as long as trust increases with it.

This is particularly important for leadership settings, which often if not always involve a leader with more formal power, and often much more power, than those led. To what degree is this dependence trusting, and hence allowing for power imbalance? To what degree is it involuntary, beckoning distrust and the desire to balance power?

THE MOST INTERESTED LEADER

As a leader or as one led, "your dependence on another person is a function of the importance of the goals the other can influence and the availability of other avenues for you to accomplish what you want."[2] What goals around task and relationship, as well as concerns around identity and face, do those led bring to the

---

2. Hocker and Wilmot, *Interpersonal Conflict*, 116.

leadership setting? In which of these specific ways do I as a leader depend on those I lead? What task and relationship goals do I have? What needs and wants around identity and face do I bring to my leadership?

The group's goals, along with those goals the individual leader brings to the group, may well be more important to the leader than to anyone else in the group. Also, members of the group may have other avenues to pursue their goals. If any of this is so, from the standpoint of dependence, the group may well have more power than its leader. The leader may be the high power party, but also the higher dependence party. Call this **the irony of the dependent leader**. This balance resonates with Waller and Hill's interpersonal *principle of least interest*, which states that the individual least invested in a personal relationship has the most power, and the person most invested must work harder to maintain it.[3]

DEPENDENCE AND THE SIX ORIENTATIONS

If I am a leader with a competing disposition, the notion that I am dependent on those I lead may well be stressful. How can I reduce my dependence, or increase theirs? This gravitates to the coercive question, how can I make them depend on me? If I am a leader with an insufficient orientation, dependence on those I lead may well be a source of anxiety. It's not a question of if they will fail me, but when. Better to just do it myself. If I am a leader with collaborating orientation or a sufficient orientation, dependence is welcome, even ideal. If I am an expansive leader, I expect to depend on those I lead. I look forward to that day when I depend on you. The coach prepares for the game, when he will depend on his players. If he doesn't, he isn't actually a coach. A flight instructor knows that she will at some point put her life in the hands of her pupil.

Regardless of the orientation a leader has toward the power of those she leads, or to state it more realistically, regardless of the mix of orientations a leader has toward any one person she leads,

---

3. Heath, *Rational Choice and Social Exchange*, 24.

leaders do depend on those they lead. In stark terms, a leader who does not depend on those she leads to achieve the group's goals is not actually a leader. She is at best a performer.

VISION, MISSION AND DEPENDENCE

Vision and mission statements, regardless of how they differ, are attempts to align the goals of the led with the goals of the leaders. When successful, the resulting mutual dependence is rewarding and synergistic. Where unsuccessful, the leader is left urging others in a direction he values, but they will follow only to the extent that it serves their individual goals.

This reveals two bracing realities for the leader. First, leaders must at some point become dependent on those they lead, or they are not actual leaders. When Jim Collins states in *Good to Great*, that leaders must "start by getting the right people on the bus, the wrong people off the bus, and the right people in the right seats," it is precisely because leaders must depend on those they lead.

Second, when it comes to vision and mission, those led are voluntarily dependent on the leader. In short, they must trust the leader. Put differently, can a leader foster any kind of meaningful group mission or vision through coercion? Can she pressure those she leads to work toward a vision?

Questions like these bring back to mind Eisenhower's guidance that *leadership is the art of getting someone else to do something you want done because he wants to do it.*

The next section, which looks at the connection between dependence and money, describes perhaps the most common and effective, though not the most artistic, means by which leaders foster dependence. But beyond this, how might a leader create a different kind of dependence by fostering a sense of belonging, shared identity, and community within her leadership setting? The discussion of identity and face in chapter 9 and the discussion of trust in chapter 10 help to ask and answer this question.

MONEY AND DEPENDENCE

As saying goes, "money is power," meaning money is resource-control power that can pay for other forms of power. Money is also a common currency of dependence. How much money is one party willing to pay another, either in a one-time fee for a service or product, or in ongoing salary and benefits? Still, if money is power, it is subject to endorsement. Statements like "Money can't buy you love" and "You couldn't pay me enough to do that" indicate as much. Dependence determines that fluctuating monetary point where demand and supply meet. A professional athlete negotiating a new contract with the team is a process of re-determining mutual dependence.

Money exchanged indicates mutual dependence. The money an employer pays an employee simultaneously indicates the employer's dependence on the employee and establishes the employee's dependence on the employer. An employee may depend upon her employment for her mortgage, her car payment, and food for her family.

DEPENDENCE AND CONSUMERISM

Dependence is of particular consideration in leadership settings where the leader is paid and those led are not. Such settings—e.g. elected-electorate, teacher-student-parent, pastor-congregation—have the potential to become skewed, originating from all the practical ways the leader depends on the leadership setting more than those led. Such leadership settings are particularly fertile ground for a consumerism. Residents of a city may look at its rising crime rate and demand of the mayor, "what are you going to do about this?" A group of parents may agree, "if the student fails, the teacher fails," ignoring their more pivotal role in their children's ability and motivation to learn. On the other hand, a presidential candidate may leverage the appeal of this consumer mindset with promises like "Elect me. I alone can fix this."

> ## You don't want to leave too, do you?
>
>> As a pastor, you wear many hats and have many 'bosses.' On a given week you may be the preacher, consoler, building-contractor, janitor, personnel manager, counselor, project organizer, mediator, fund-raiser, vision-caster, and peacekeeper. No pastor can always "perform well" in even half of these areas.[4]
>
>> "You do not want to leave too, do you?" Jesus asked the Twelve. (John 6:67)
>
> No one word captures the practical, day-to-day challenges of church leadership more, or more frankly, than dependence. Any legitimate power, authority, expert power can be more than offset by low dependence. Those they seek to lead can just leave.
>
> And because of their self-perception of low power, members often don't understand the consequences of their actions. Gossiping, back-biting, and the informal coalitions these build: these are not seen as harmful. How do my actions matter?
>
> And sources of power church members wield are so easily converted to coercive power. They can *vote with their wallets* and *vote with their feet*. This is mirrored in church leaders' temptation to lower their own dependence; to see members primarily as "numbers, nickels, and noses." In short, a high-low dependence relationship can become self-fulfilling.
>
> Yes, church leaders often depend on this setting for their mortgage and groceries. But as much or more than other settings, church leaders can come to highly, even impossibly, depend on this setting for their identity. A family not coming for a while, or someone playing with his phone during a sermon, can be crushing. Self protection, or even abuse of power, only makes sense.
>
> But, except for the cell-phone, Jesus faced all these challenges too. And his dialog-based, give-and-take leadership style, with all its vulnerability, enabled him to build shared identity, foster belonging, and create a durable community that has withstood great internal and external challenges.
>
> 4. Slagle, "Three Irrational Beliefs"

CHAPTER 9

Face and Identity

Definitions of leadership, as Chapter 2 notes, focus on either desired outcomes, or influencing others, or the connection between both these goals. This acknowledged, leaders and led are keenly and constantly motivated by identity-related questions like *How do I want others to see me?* and *Is my work respected?* and *Does my job line up with my ideals?* Further, face concerns—*Are you talking down me? Would you say that to me if I was white?* and *Don't roll your eyes at me.*—can stymie leadership settings. This chapter explores how face and identity concerns can impact leadership settings as it examines specific dynamics like *negative face, positive face, face threat, face gain, shared identity, culture, and normative power.*

NEGATIVE AND POSITIVE FACE

Within their oft-cited *Politeness Theory*, Brown and Levinson define face as "the public self-image every member wants to claim for himself."[1] Keenly-felt interests such as respect, esteem, validation, honor, and dignity reflect the vital importance of face to each of us. So do the consequences of *face loss*, e.g., embarrassment, invalidation, dishonor, and shame. Face is so important to each of us that

---

1. Brown & Levinson, *Politeness*, 61.

we carefully and mutually steward one another's face as we interact. "In general, people cooperate in maintaining face in interaction, such cooperation being based on mutual vulnerability of face."[2] We say "Please," "Thank you," and "Excuse me," and we drill our kids to do so as well. All of these learned, *face-saving* gestures indicate the sensitive, delicate, constant nature of face concerns. Am I being condescending in how I give you instructions? Was I short with you? One person making another feel unappreciated, taken for granted, or merely uncomfortable threatens face. *This mutual face concern may be the biggest reason power is difficult to discuss.*

Brown and Levinson differentiate between **negative face** and **positive face**. My *positive face* concerns encompass my need for others to see my self-image favorably as we communicate, "crucially including the desire for that self-image to be appreciated and approved of."[3] Positive face covers a vast spectrum of conscious and unconscious concerns we have as we interact. Do you respect me? What impression am I making? Do I have something caught in my teeth? Are you seeing me as insightful, confident, trustworthy?

Negative face asks the same "Do you respect me?" question from a subtly different angle. Negative face reflects my desire for "freedom of action and freedom from imposition."[4] My negative face concerns lead me to ask: Are you demonstrating respect for me in how you are imposing on me? Did I say "Pardon the interruption" before interrupting, or did I just barge in? Do you appreciate how important my time is? When I honk my horn at you, it's about negative face: you are carelessly interfering with me.

FACE AND THE SIX ORIENTATIONS

Awareness of face concerns is perhaps the most sensitive means by which to assess my orientation toward your power as we interact. My sense of ease or comfort when you argue a point, or my head

2. Ibid.
3. Brown and Levinson, *Politeness*, 61.
4. Ibid.

nod in agreement, indicate a collaborating orientation, for example, just as the stress I may feel, and my pursed lips, may indicate a competing orientation within this instance of interaction. Cutting you off as mid-sentence is a symptom of a competing orientation. If I have a competitive disposition toward you, I may put you down, or roll my eyes as you talk, in a deliberate attempt to cause you face loss.

NEGATIVE FACE VERSUS LEADERSHIP?

Within leadership settings, negative face concerns merit particular scrutiny because they, by their very definition, run contrary to acts of power and leadership. Compare the following four definitions:

> Negative face: the want of every "competent adult member" that his actions be unimpeded by others.[5] Also, "freedom of action and freedom from imposition."[6]

> Power is the ability to change the behavior of others.
>
> —*Robert Vecchio*

> A leader takes people where they want to go. A great leader takes people where they don't necessarily want to go, but ought to be.
>
> —*Roslyn Carter*

> The task of the leader is to get his people from where they are to where they have not been.
>
> —*Henry Kissinger*

Note how the description of negative face pulls in the opposite direction of these definitions of power and leadership. This comparison lends credence to Ashforth and Mael's contention that workplace resistance is often a means to protect or enhance identity.[7]

5. Ibid. 63.
6. Ibid. 61.
7. Ashforth and Mael, "Power of Resistance," 97–98.

While it could be said that negative face concerns automatically oppose leadership, this understanding is inaccurate and unnecessarily contentious. Indeed, leadership settings come with the expectation of being imposed upon, or should. An army private expects to take orders and carry them out. A waiter expects to wait tables. "Some task goals (e.g., getting people out of a burning building) are so dominant that face concerns may drop by the wayside. In some cases joining a group means accepting someone's authority (e.g., joining the army) regardless of face concerns."[8] Restating a point from the previous chapter differently, any leadership setting that does not impose upon those led, i.e., does not obligate them and depend upon them to further its purposes, is not actually a leadership setting. It is instead, at best, a performance.

A more constructive understanding of the seemingly contrary relationship between leadership and negative face is this: people naturally want to be respected in how they are imposed upon by leaders. Those definitions of power and leadership that emphasize relationship (see Table 2.1) address this. The leader who, for example, authentically communicates respect and appreciation as he leads, especially when he imposes in unexpected ways, stewards the face concerns of those led. This contrasts the leader who, perhaps because she is focused only on her desired outcomes, does not respect the time and interests of those she leads.

FACE LOSS

Understanding *face loss* clarifies why face and identity concerns can quickly and deeply disrupt leadership settings. "People are said to *lose face* when they are treated in such a way that their identity claims are challenged or ignored."[9] When I lose face I may feel offended, insulted, slighted, demeaned, ashamed, or stepped on. I may experience embarrassment, indignation, humiliation, or perceive disrespect, dishonor or disregard. Whenever someone

8. Brown, email interview, October 2013.
9. Folger et al., *Working Through Conflict*, 176.

experiences intense anger, a safe question to ask is, "How were that person's face and/or identity concerns abraded?"

And if a person's face can be lost, it can also be deliberately attacked, such as when that person is belittled, scorned, ridiculed, taunted, mocked, despised, or rejected. The intensity of these forms of face loss illustrates how crucial face and identity are to each of us. Further, these responses are usually in the moment and retrospective: face loss often comes as an unwelcome, disorienting surprise.

FACE VERSUS TASK GOALS

Examples abound in which face concerns and face loss overwhelm leadership settings. A rock-star CEO resigns amidst charges of sexual harassment from female employees. An Air Force commander faces court-martial for conduct unbecoming an officer. A state university experiences a 35% drop in enrollment, and is forced to cut hundreds of positions, after allegations of racism ignite ugly, televised on-campus protests.

Consider two other practical examples of face loss trumping desired outcomes and official duties: First, on September 22, 1842, Illinois state legislator Abraham Lincoln took time out from duties of state, and any concern for his wedding twelve days later, to duel Illinois state auditor James Shields with broadswords, the weapon of Lincoln's choosing. The duel, averted at the last moment, was Shields' idea after a critique by Lincoln in the local paper was augmented beyond good taste by Lincoln's fiancé, Mary Todd. Examples such as this, even on an official level, in which concerns around face and identity overwhelm task goals, are both troubling and easy to find. A second example comes from the Old Testament, and is offered here because it is simply too illustrative and amusing to forgo. It describes Naaman, a commander in the army of Aram, who travels to see someone who can heal his leprosy:

> So Naaman went with his horses and chariots and stopped at the door of Elisha's house. Elisha sent a messenger to say to him, "Go, wash yourself seven times in the Jordan, and your flesh will be restored and you will

be cleansed." But Naaman went away angry and said, "I thought that he would surely come out to me and stand and call on the name of the Lord his God, wave his hand over the spot and cure me of my leprosy. Are not Abana and Pharpar, the rivers of Damascus, better than all the waters of Israel? Couldn't I wash in them and be cleansed?" So he turned and went off in a rage. Naaman's servants went to him and said, "My father, if the prophet had told you to do some great thing, would you not have done it? How much more, then, when he tells you, 'Wash and be cleansed'!" (2 Kings 5:9–13)

Among the many interesting aspects of this example is that the keenly desired outcome goal, the removal of leprosy, which Namaan travelled far to attain, is refused because of the face loss Namaan experienced while interacting with Elisha.

FACE GAIN

Brown and Levinson point out that face can be "enhanced"[10] in interaction as well as lost. One person can bring about *face gain* by asking another to "'Tell me what you think" or "Elaborate on that." All of these actions endorse another person's power, and boost that person's positive face. One person may impose upon another in a way that enhances their negative face as well: "You're taller than I am; can you reach that for me?" or "You explained this well; tell them what you told me."

In each of these examples, including mere listening, one person imposes on another in a way that enhances that person's face. Each builds up, raises up, endorses, elevates, validates, demonstrates trust, empowers, and encourages another. And each, along the way, furthers task and relational goals.

But these bouyant examples must be diligently contrasted with that person, leader or led, who flatters, *butters up*, or *kisses up*. Such a person enhances someone else's face solely to bring about her own desired outcomes.

10. Brown and Levinson, *Politeness*, 61.

HIGH POWER AND FACE THREAT—A FIRST LOOK

The risk of losing face, or *face threat*, increases in power-imbalanced settings, such as most if not all leadership settings.

> The greatest potential face threat is found when there is great social distance between the parties, the listener has more power than the speaker, and there is a great degree of imposition placed on the communicative request or act.[11]

Consider an example: Steve is presenting a cost-saving initiative to a group of four peers, and Maria disagrees with his logic. "Pardon me," she interrupts and describes a critical flaw in his strategy. Now, how might face threat increase for Maria if Steve is her COO, rather than her peer.

Chapter 13 will address face threat and power imbalance from another important angle as it describes **the irony of Henry V.**

POWER IMBALANCE AND FACE GAIN

If the power imbalance between leaders and led increases face threat, it can also increase face gain. One colleague saying "Great idea" to another after a meeting brings some level of face gain, but the chairman saying the same thing means much more.

This example illustrates positive face gain. Leaders can affect negative face gain as well, simply by acknowledging the imposition placed upon those led in a way that demonstrates respect. An army commander telling his troops that they are heading into extreme danger honors them and motivates them with his honesty. John F. Kennedy demonstrated how compelling such an imposition can be when stating, "My fellow Americans, ask not what your country can do for you, ask what you can do for your country."

---

11. Folger et al., *Working Through Conflict*, 175.

IDENTITY, FACE, AND COERCION

The more concern I have for my social identity, i.e. how I want others to see me, the more power others can have over me. What value do I place on your approval, and how can you leverage this? Consider the coercive power of the following identity-related questions:

- Are you smart enough to figure this out?
- You're not chicken, are you?
- Are you man enough?

Each of these questions is my bid to gain power by placing your identity under my discretion. If you agree with my question, then how you are seen becomes subject to my criteria. Each of these questions uses your identity coercively against you. Consider three more involved questions:

- Was it a mistake to depend on you?
- Do you expect me to settle for this?
- Did I raise you to treat me this way?

These are double-bind, doubly coercive questions that establish that you have already caused me face loss. And now your face and identity are on the line. Those are my toes you just stepped on. If you are a polite person, then your face loss at causing my face loss may be greater than my face loss. You may instinctively feel shame and some level of obligation to make amends, likely by doing exactly as I wish.

These questions demonstrate how my willingness to proclaim face loss in polite company can be a potent form of coercion. A person may loudly *make a martyr of herself, lick her wounds, say "Woe is me"* or *feel sorry for herself* as a means of coercing desired outcomes. Further, I have an out if you fail: I can smartly say that I expected as little. Indeed, how many leaders have, while minimizing their own face risk, accomplished extraordinary outcomes with face-threatening questions like" "Where are your guts?" "I thought you had what it took?" and "You're not going to take that lying down, are you?"

IDENTITY AND RESISTANCE

Acts of resistance are often motivated by identity concerns. Rosa Parks quietly refusing to move from her seat was a stance for her identity, as was the lone, slender protester stopping a line of tanks in Tiananmen Square. A teenager arguing with his mom over just about anything is likely trying to establish or process his own identity, as is a vandal painting a swastika on the side of a synagogue. In all of these widely varying examples, resistance is motivated by identity concerns. "Resistance is often used to forge or sustain valued conceptions of self in the face of situational pressures to do otherwise. At one extreme, resistance may be used to defend a relatively complete social identity. . . . At the other extreme, resistance may be used to defend idiosyncratic aspects of one's personal identity."[12] Resistance may be for healthy, even altruistic motives, or an effort to bolster one's identity, or a basic means to competitively gain power.

RESISTING EXPANSIVE LEADERSHIP

While identity and face impact any leadership setting, they can define expansive leadership settings most tangibly. Specifically, expansive leadership settings exist to change the identities of those led. Anyone coming into a classroom does so precisely to be imposed upon and improved upon; to be more tomorrow than she is today. But many students enter the classroom not expecting or wanting identity change, especially if they are there involuntarily. They recognize the empowerment taking place only as effort and imposition. "When am I ever going to use this stuff?" "When will this class be over?"

Expansive leaders—teachers, coaches, and mentors—may find themselves facing a two-fold resistance. First, a student may resist as a way to establish or enhance her own identity. The classclown, or the student who argues just to appear smart, resists for his personal identity gain. This is the same resistance any leader

---

12. Ashforth and Mael, "Power of Resistance," 92.

FACE AND IDENTITY

may experience. But in an expansive setting, resistance may also be to the growth that setting seeks to instill. Expansive settings expose my identity to new growth. Given the vulnerability and identity threat inherent in that growth, I may be that much more likely to instinctively resist.

Hence the leader in an expansive, learning environment faces a unique challenge: getting those lead to accept the identity change and face risk that goes with learning.

The expansive leader and expansively led must individually understand and mutually agree, perhaps by conscious choice or agreement or covenant or cultural expectation as the relationship begins, that the purpose of the leadership setting is to expand the power of the led. Expansive leadership settings exist to increase the power of those led, but each person's identity and negative face concerns can hinder or even derail this process. In short: Is he coachable? Is she teachable? Is he correctable? These questions, though they outwardly address task goals and relationship goals, are questions of identity and face. Will the one led, for his own sake, voluntarily submit to the one seeking to empower him?

The concept of identity change brings expansive leadership and other types of leadership into sharper contrast. A collaborating leader may have the luxury of agreeing that no identity change is necessary. "I like you just the way you are." An expansive leader may well begin here, and indeed should, but can't stay. A competing leader, in even stronger contrast, sees any expanded power by others as her loss of power, and a loss of identity with it. For the competing leader, mere submission as ideal. However, the expansive leader sees submitting as ideal, a necessary step toward empowerment of the individual and the coordinated power of the group.

REFERENT LEADERSHIP AND IDENTITY

Referent influence, referent power, and referent leadership, introduced in chapter 3, have a unique connection with identity. But each differs distinctly. The example of the popular football player illustrates this. Perhaps due to charming personality or special abilities, one football player may end up with more fans then another. This is unintentional referent influence. Fans may choose to buy his jersey and gain identity from placing his name on their backs. But of this player hawks a car in a TV commercial, this is an effort in deliberate referent power to influence a transaction. Player and car company are deliberately leveraging his identity.

The collective identity formed around referent influence and referent power can be compelling, as the fan bases of rock stars and sports teams attest. Stadiums are built to accommodate collective identity. However, outsiders may look askance at that avid community and its shared identity. Further, those who share a competing identity, such as another sports team's fan base or another political candidate's constituents, will reasonably view this group's power competitively.

But referent leadership goes further. The *referent* or *charismatic leader* draws upon others' devotion intentionally, as a means of purposive, transformative influence. A referent leader can say, "If you love me, you will do as I say." Max Weber argued that truly referent or charismatic leaders are historically rare, "and treated as endowed with supernatural, superhuman, or at least exceptional powers or qualities. These are not accessible to the ordinary person, but regarded as of divine origin or as exemplary, and on the basis of them the individual concerned is treated as a leader."[13] A good test of a referent leader is the use of the term *follower*. A referent leader can refer to those she leads as *followers* to their faces, as affirmation. A referent leader can make imposing statements like, "If you wish to be my followers, you must ... " Those led by a referent leader call themselves followers as a form of shared identity. In referent leadership settings, uniquely, the term *follower* is empowering.

Referent leaders and their followers are studied and discussed at length, often with troubling conclusions. Narcissism, delusions, and mental illness are common assessments, along with intensely coercive, even violent methods of control. Sometimes the leader and followers die by their own hand. Rare is the referent leader who does not sooner or later earn infamy.

13. Weber, *On Charisma and Institution Building*, 48.

SHARED IDENTITY FOSTERS NORMATIVE POWER

My identity—how others see me—is impacted by how others see people like me. How am I associated with others? With whom do I identify? With whom do others identify me? My nationality, my skin color, my alma mater, and my favorite baseball team can all be sources of shared identity. The identity I share with you leads me to ask, "How do your attitudes and actions reflect on me?" A child's performance on the soccer field, for example, affects her parents' identity. A person whose identity embarrasses the rest of her family is called a *black sheep*. Someone may refuse to join a group because she doesn't want to be associated with that group's *lunatic fringe*. An individual's identity is often impacted, for better or worse, by the people connected with her.

Normative power, introduced in chapter 2, is a group's power over individuals who value that group, who want to belong to it, who want to share that group's identity. Varied and valued terms like *peer pressure, corporate culture, conformity,* and *outcast* allude to the potent sway of normative power, and the importance of belonging. Peter Drucker's statement that "Culture eats strategy for breakfast"[14] reflects how normative power and shared identity can overwhelm even formally established task goals. Ashforth and Mael capture the underlying potency of normative power and shared identity, in part by framing them in terms of coercive potential:

> What makes normative control so insidious is that, when complete, it is experienced not as externally imposed but as internalized and freely chosen... It insinuates itself into one's workplace identity such that to resist it is to be war with oneself.... It is this fusion of self and organization that makes normative control so appealing to organizations.[15]

Normative power—with the shared identity and belonging it both offers and implicitly threatens to remove—can be intensely

---

14. Braun, "It's the Culture, Stupid," line 5.
15. Ashforth and Mael, "Power of Resistance," 93.

Ironies Leaders Navigate

coercive. Examples include the peer pressure of a fraternity initiation ritual requiring an incoming pledge to drink a six pack of beer in six minutes, or a mortgage firm associate using unethical accounting methods, because "thems the rules here."

But as Hocker and Wilmot describe about power in general, normative power is not in itself right or wrong; it just is. Normative power is heard in firm statements like: "You never leave a man behind," "We the People," and " . . . the land of the free and home of the brave."

Would You Give Me a Drink of Water?

Jesus and the plucky Samaritan woman in John 4 demonstrate the extreme face and identity dynamics stewarded within The Church. A Jewish rabbi encounters a lone female, derided by her people, who are derided by the Jews. Face threat would be greater only if she was a leper too. She has every reason to look down, perhaps abandon drawing her water, and depart. But he finds the one way to overcome the threat he poses to her: her asks her for a favor. He imposes in a way that gives her power and face gain. Ironically, he makes himself unclean with the request.

Some rapport established, she jibes, "You are a Jew and I am a Samaritan woman. How can you ask me for a drink?" Jesus jests back, basically saying *if you only knew*. He is more powerful than she can imagine, he explains, enough to offer her eternal life. He practically dares her to accept this "living water." (John 4:10) And she does.

But with belonging comes identity-shattering honesty. Jesus knows all about her: "You are right when you say you have no husband. The fact is, you have had five husbands, and the man you now have is not your husband." (John 4:17–18a) With Jesus she finds herself totally vulnerable, yet unconditionally secure. He knew all these sordid details when he offered her eternity with him.

Her personal identity secure and her social identity no longer dependent upon her townsfolk, she marches back into their midst. There she boldly interferes, commanding, "Come see a man who told me everything I ever did. Could this be the Christ?"(John 4:29) And they do. This scorned woman becomes, by any definition, their leader. And so changed is she that she is safe holding up her own blotched identity, *everything I ever did,* as a means of influence.

Church leaders must steward all this woman embodies. Much power and freedom comes from seeing oneself as Jesus does. And he can make a fellow leader out of anyone, regardless of how others see her or how she sees herself.

It Is No Longer I Who Live ...

Most organizations focus on task outcomes. Manufacturers manufacture. Hospitals help sick people. The Church focuses on identity outcomes: how should I see myself, and how should I see others relative to myself: "The greatest among you will be your servant." (Matthew 23:11) "Love your neighbor as yourself." (Mark 12:31b). Addressing this focus from a different angle, Jesus chastens those leaders who lead primarily to advance their own identities:

> Everything they do is done for people to see: They make their phylacteries wide and the tassels on their garments long; they love the place of honor at banquets and the most important seats in the synagogues. (Matthew 23:5–6)

What drives me more than how I want others to see me? What resists God's view of me more than how I view myself? Jesus' outrageous intent is to confront and change that which I cherish most: my identity.

"Therefore, if anyone is in Christ, he is a new creation; the old has gone, the new has come!" (2 Cor 5:17). Note the bracing identity transformation in:

Redemption	Salvation	Forgiven	Forgiveness	Baptism
Reconciliation	Conviction	Renewal	Freedom	Repentance
Sanctification	Purification	Peace	Humility	Rebirth
Consecration	Joy	Correction	Rebuke	Confession

But transformation is necessarily not our religious duty to God. Instead we actively allow God to bring it about in us:

> When we despair of gaining inner transformation through human powers of will and determination we are open to a wonderful new realization: inner righteousness is a gift from God to be graciously received. The needed change within us is God's work, not ours.[16]

Church leaders face the challenge of shepherding this stunning identity transformation process within community.

16. Foster, *Celebration of Discipline*, 6–7.

Everything I Ever Did!

Returning to the woman leading others back to the well, she has spoken of her derided former self, *everything I ever did*, with a forgiven detachment. How she refers to her past argues that she agrees with everyone's assessment. But with her identity transformed, this is now merely part of her testimony, describing her past but no longer defining her presence. Her former disrepute is now an ironic source of power.

The identity transformation modeled by this woman, and the freedom that results, permeates the Gospels themselves. The Gospel writers routinely describe themselves in a most unflattering light. Peter, for example, is widely regarded as the editor-in-chief behind the first three gospels, yet these detail his many awkward blunders. And John, who refers to himself as *the disciple whom Jesus loved* (John 13:23), will never call himself *the humble or the self-aware*, given that he takes time out from describing Jesus' resurrection to note for the record that he outran Peter to the empty tomb. (John 20:3)

One obscure argument that Scripture is indeed authored according to God's purposes is simply that its human writers would likely have neglected to include these many embarrassing accounts of themselves, if left to their own preferences. And anyone revising these works later with an eye toward improving them would almost certainly have removed these more discrediting descriptions of the key characters. Is chronicling your group's ongoing "who's the greatest" argument really an effective way to draw others to join it?

Regardless, the disciples demonstrate the consequences of the identity transformation that Jesus calls forth. The Church, modelled by the very first leaders within it, is to be a community of individuals who take themselves lightly, perhaps even humorously, looking back with acknowledgement, but also with forgiven detachment, at *everything I ever did*.

> ## Lord, Don't You Care...?
>
> > "The greatest potential face threat is found when there is great social distance between the parties, the listener has more power than the speaker, and there is a great degree of imposition placed on the communicative request or act."[17]
>
> > "Lord, don't you care that my sister has left me to do the work by myself? Tell her to help me!" (Luke 10:40b)
>
> Martha is a Jewish hostess in her own home, likely serving mostly male guests, including a popular rabbi. Given the immense social distance in this setting, face threat would be greater only if Martha were to confront Jesus with some shrill demand. Which she does. Scripture does not record whether Martha is waving a dirty skillet at Jesus while interrupting, but it seems fitting.
>
> Like so many church volunteers who will come after her, Martha has been faithfully laboring according to her gifts. But now she is feeling slighted, even taken for granted. Few instances of face loss sting more. So she creates a triangulation template employed in church for centuries to come. Wrapping her identity wound in a task goal, she takes her problem with her sister to the leader. Martha publically "asks" Jesus a doubly coercive, double bind question, "Don't you care..." What answer can he give? Here is the Scriptural equivalent of asking, "Does this dress make me look fat?" This is a manipulative work of art.
>
> Still, what about the immense face threat? How could she speak this honestly and angrily to Jesus? Who does she think he is? Asked differently, what has this leader done to make himself so safe and approachable across such a wide social distance?
>
> Still, the Church has a word for brusque demands like Martha's: prayer. This happens all the time. This describes any instance of intercession or even prayerful anger, and certainly any request for forgiveness. What has God done to make those inside and outside The Church feel safe, rightly, imposing in this way?
>
> 17. Folger et al. *Working Through Conflict*, 175.

Do You Love Me?

Peter's identity is in tatters. It began a three nights ago, when he loyally proclaimed that he would die before denying Jesus, and Jesus predicted otherwise. Soon after, Jesus had to fix an ear Peter cut off in a fisherman's display of swordsmanship. By dawn Peter had fulfilled Jesus' promise, denying him three times. Jesus looked him in the eye the third time. Then Peter watched everyone else take turns vilifying Jesus in every way, especially violently. Jesus was whipped, mocked, crowned with thorns, stripped, crucified, etcetera. Even the man on the next cross over ridiculed him. Finally, God himself forsook him. Good Friday observes not only Jesus' physical suffering and death, but the slow crushing of his identity and face. He was made nothing.

But now he's back, again eye-to-eye with Peter. Another leader might call this meeting to humiliate and fire him. But instead Jesus has a few questions, three in fact, but all about the same. Do you love me? (See John 21) Each shames Peter more. But Jesus is not asking. Jesus is reminding Peter to recognize what he already knows. Peter loves Jesus. Peter loves Jesus. Peter loves Jesus unconditionally. In the light of the risen Christ, Peter's faithfulness will be powered not by his own loyalty but on their mutual love. Knowing this, Jesus speaks audaciously. First, the Good Shepherd entrusts this so far unreliable man with the care of his sheep. Second, he foretells Peter's death. Peter will be crucified for his loving loyalty to Jesus Christ.

Loyalty is an admirable form of endorsement. It looks and feels like love, and ideally is a symptom of it. But as Peter demonstrates, loyalty can act independently, under its own power, serving one's own identity. Loyalty does not require relationship or intimacy. I can be intensely, even mortally loyal to a code or a belief or a religion. And where love brings out patience and kindness, religious loyalty can approve hatred, even violence. One challenge church leaders face is escorting people like Peter beyond an impressive loyalty to Jesus, and deeper into a loving, sanctifying, often tattered, sometimes excruciating, but eye-to-eye relationship *with* him.

CHAPTER 10

Trust and Distrust

Do you trust me? Do you distrust me? Do you trust me both more and less than I trust you? In ongoing relationships, leadership settings especially, the answer to all these questions is, "Yes, always." Leaders and led constantly and simultaneously trust and distrust one another in many ways, each fluidly increasing and decreasing. The consultants on a software implementation team may trust their project manager to coordinate deliverables and client-team communications smoothly, while maintaining a healthy distrust that that same PM will a pull a team member off the project immediately if that person is not dressed according to client standards while on-site.

How power works in relationship depends on the trust and distrust within it, and how trust and distrust works in relationship depends on how power works within it. For example, trust enables the use of some forms of power, such as expertise, which in turn impacts trust. Likewise, over-reliance on distrust-based power, i.e. punishments, reprimands, berating poor performance, can reasonably lead to general distrust. That said, a leader's thoughtful use of distrust-based power can actually foster high trust.

Several factors describing trust and distrust are summarized at the beginning of this chapter, and then explored in detail. (Note that this summary does not match the order in which these concepts are explored.)

- Trust differs diametrically from distrust, i.e., distrust is not the same as low trust.
- Both distrust and trust can be parsed into (at least) two forms: *calculus based* and *identification based*.[1]
- Calculus-based trust is the impersonal trust in someone to perform as expected, such as a clerk at a drive-thru window. Identification-based trust is a deeper trust seen in friendships, family, etc.
- Combining the previous points creates four relationship-defining dynamics: calculus-based trust (CBT), calculus-based distrust (CBD), identification-based trust (IBT), and identification-based distrust (IBD).[2]
- Most ongoing relationships, especially leader-led relationships, are a constant intertwined fabric involving these four.
- Trust is voluntary endorsement of trust-based power. Distrust is involuntary endorsement of coercive power.
- All forms of trust and distrust can be violated, with differing effects on the relationship. Violating IBT, for example, is likely to be much more defining and damaging than violating CBT.

TRUST VERSUS DISTRUST

Trust and distrust differ in a mirrored, opposite way. Trust is "a confident *positive* expectation regarding another's conduct," and distrust is "a confident *negative* expectation regarding another's conduct."[3] My trust in you is my confident expectation that you will benefit my interests, i.e. will help me achieve my goals. My

---

1. Lewicki and Wiethoff, "Trust, Trust Development, and Trust Repair," 88–89.
2. Ibid., 92–93.
3. Ibid.

distrust in you is my confident expectation that you will hinder or harm my interests, if you need or want to, to achieve your goals.

Hence, low trust is very different from distrust. Low trust is low confidence that you will benefit my interests. Distrust is confidence that you will bring harm to my interests.

TRUST, DISTRUST, AND ENDORSEMENT

From the standpoint of power and endorsement, trust is the voluntary endorsement that another has trust-based power. Distrust, in contrast, is the confident expectation that another will use distrust-based power. A student may trust what his teacher explains to him in class, and distrust that she will send him to the office if he is unruly. Further, he may have high distrust in the dean to call his parents, but low distrust that his parents will reprimand him.

Hence, distrust is the involuntary endorsement of another person's distrust-based power. An employee may show up to work on time not because she wants to, but because she is certain her boss will fire her if she doesn't. A motorist may refrain from running the red light at a specific intersection because he knows this one has a traffic camera installed.

EMPLOYING AL CAPONE

To restate *the irony of Al Capone*: formal leaders often control both trust-based and distrust-based sources of power. A leader's effectiveness is determined in small or large part by how carefully she balances these. This book's introduction argued that a leader's use of power is an artistic endeavor. Few examples support this argument more than leaders' constant balancing of trust-and distrust-based power.

Assessing the Use of Distrust-Based Power

Many questions can be asked to help assess this balance. Six of the most basic are presented here.

First, what specific types of distrust-based power does a formal leader actually have? Does a leader actually have power to punish, or bring about negative outcomes for those she leads?

Second, does it work? Does it cause changed behavior? Does the threat of this punishment keep someone from doing what you don't want them to? Does this punishment keep them from doing it again? Does the threat of prison keep a person from committing a crime? And will that person commit that crime or another when they are free again?

Third, how predominantly does the leader rely upon distrust-based power? For example, the classroom in which a teacher cultivates interpersonal linkage power but avoids using her authority (i.e., to confiscate cell phones) differs greatly from a classroom in which a teacher relies solely on her right to assign detention as a means to manage classroom conduct, and relates in a way that does not foster trust-based power.

Fourth, does the group recognize the leader's use of distrust-based power as beneficial to the group? Does the class recognize that the teacher is using his distrust-based power to improve their learning environment? Does the rest of the community believe the person going to jail got a fair trial and a fair punishment? In short, does the group trust the leader's use of distrust-based power? Call this **the irony of trusting distrust.**

A fifth question is perhaps the best mark of expansive leadership: Do those punished agree with this process? Do they, or will they, agree they got what they deserved? Do they have every opportunity to grow from this response? If so, this punishment is an example of expansive correction, and trust can grow from it. This is an ideal outcome, but distrust-based power may be used with great care and still not produce this result.

A sixth question regarding the use of distrust-based power also provides a good example of ecological power: has the leader prepared the group for the leader's use of distrust-based power? Do they know the rules? Do they recognize when he will use this power and why, perhaps to the point that they police themselves in ways that benefit the group?

DIFFERENT FORMS OF TRUST

If trust and distrust, including how they often coexist in the same relationship, were not complicated enough already, Lewicki and Weithoff further differentiate each into two forms. ***Calculus-based trust*** (CBT) "tends to occur most frequently in professional, non-intimate, task-oriented relationships."[4] It is the trust placed in an accounting firm to provide a reliable audit, or in a pharmacy to fill a prescription. It is the trust placed in another party to perform as promised. Many companies live or die on the CBT their customers place in them.

Identification-based trust (IBT) is trust on a personal, emotional, identity level. "IBT is grounded in perceived compatibility of values, common goals, and positive emotional attachment to each other."[5] IBT is the trust we place in loved ones, those we agree with, and whose values we share. We are "like-minded." "This mutual understanding is developed to a point that each person can effectively act for the other. . . . A true affirmation of the strength of IB TRUST between parties can be found when one party acts for the other even more zealously than the other might demonstrate, such as when a good friend dramatically defends you against a minor insult."[6] A shared identity forms with those in whom I place IBT. "A collective identity develops; we empathize strongly with the other and incorporate parts of their psyche into our identity."[7]

Calculus-based distrust (CBD) also involves impersonal transactions within relationships, and involves the "confident

4. Ibid., 89.
5. Ibid., 93.
6. Ibid., 89.
7. Ibid., 90.

negative expectations regarding another's conduct." Calculus-based distrust is how a speeding motorist feels about a state trooper, or a tardy employee feels toward the manager who can fire him.

Identification-based distrust (IBD) "is grounded in perceived *incompatibility* of values, *dissimilar* goals, and *negative* emotional attachment to the other."[8] One party with IBD toward another believes that what she values—e.g., identity goals, face concerns, or general well-being—is threatened or endangered by another party. A shift manager may have high CBT that her supervisor will pay her, but firm IBD toward him because he mocks her political views, and because he doesn't remember her that name is Aubrey, not Audrey.

Lewicki and Weithoff stress that CBT, IBT, CBD, and IBD can mutually define any ongoing relationship. For example, they describe a relationship with high CBT, low CBD, low IBT, and low IBD as "a good working relationship."[9] In contrast, a relationship with low CBT, high CBD, high IBT, and low IBD is one they summarize as, "I love you but you're a flake."[10]

A vivid example of how IB trust and IB distrust can coexist is seen in Ken Blanchard's depiction of the "one-minute reprimand," which describes how to change the behavior of another while validating her face and identity.[11] Leadership priorities like the ones Blanchard presents illustrate a key aspect of the irony of trusting distrust: if the leader has earned IB trust, this allows her to expansively employ IB distrust.

BUILDING CB TRUST, STENGTHENING IB TRUST

Building calculus-based trust is straight-forward. Just deliver as expected. Keep your promises. Meet obligations. No surprises. For some groups, especially business organizations, success depends ultimately on building CBT.

8. Ibid., 93.
9. Ibid., 94.
10. Ibid.
11. Blanchard, *One Minute Manager*, 30.

In contrast, we build IBT through the give and take of relationship. To earn your IBtrust, I must demonstrate that I identify with you, that I respect you, that I hear you. Your identity is safe with me. In brief or passing interactions, this looks like saying "please" and "thank you," and respecting your personal space.

But within deeper, more meaningful relationships, we strengthen IB trust by stretching it, and exercising it, like a muscle. We push each other. I must test whether my identity is actually safe. Durable, truly high IB trust relationships are forged through candid community. "We've had our share of arguments." "I've gotten in her face, and she's gotten in mine." "We've both had to apologize."

This reveals from another angle how the most trusting relationships involve a healthy dose of IB distrust. "He tells me things I need to hear, but don't want to." In some ways, my identity is not safe around this person. "I respect you, so I am going to be very honest with you."

This kind of frank relationship is vital, because my identity must change. We call this growth, maturation, learning. How I see myself and how I want others to see me should be different today than they were 10 years ago, or I am not growing. This is particularly true for leaders. No leader should want to be the same leader she was 10 years ago.

As noted earlier, this aggressive blending of IB trust and IB distrust is particularly important in expansive leadership settings, which gauge their success on growth. The best expansive leaders are known for the ways they challenged and stretched and strengthened the identities of those they led. Consider for example some of the expansive, identity focused, identity changing leadership given by Coach John Wooden, widely regarded as the greatest basketball coach of all time:

> If you're not making mistakes, then you're not doing anything. I'm positive that a doer makes mistakes.
>
> Make a decision! Failure to act is often the biggest failure of all.

Be more concerned with your character than your reputation, because your character is what you really are, while your reputation is merely what others think you are.

You can't let praise or criticism get to you. It's a weakness to get caught up in either one.

Us Against Them: Leading by Shared Distrust

Shared identity and identification-based trust make sense together. One comes with the other. We are "soul-sisters," "brothers in arms." I have your back.

However, shared identity based on shared distrust can be a much more powerful force. If you distrust the same people I do, based on their political views, gender, nationality or race, we may identify with each other bigly. We share the same concerns about "preserving our way of life." Racism, nationalism, sexism tribalism, among other isms, are founded upon IB distrust.

Groups can galvanize community around shared identification-based distrust of another group. Cold War Russia versus Cold War U.S.; Tutsi versus Hutu; Democrats versus Republicans; Black Lives Matter versus All Lives Matter; us versus them. Groups like the KKK and ISIS depend on high IB distrust for their existence. White supremacists, the the alt-right movement, and Antifa are fueled by IB distrust. And they generate IB distrust, understandably, as they work to achieve their purposes.

Further, some leaders leverage shared IB distrust to rally others. Mudslinging political ads strive to intentionally influence by igniting IB distrust, as do labels like "Lyin' Ted" and "Crooked Hillary."

Beyond the entrenched divisiveness, shared IB distrust merits several cautions. First, it enables and even encourages fundamental attribution error on a group level. Whatever "they" do simply must be wrong. Whatever we do must be right. A competing orientation toward that "them" is motivating, even patriotic.

Second, opposition to another group based on identity differences may become a more energizing, directive force than that group's principles independent of opposition. We know what we stand against but not what we stand for. Third, cooperation and compromise with the other group may be seen as weakness or betrayal. That political party is the enemy. Hence, both sides risk sacrificing the opportunity to become more powerful together. Finally, such groups may come to rely on entrenched opposition for their shared identity. We run the risk of becoming anti-Republicans and anti-Democrats, instead of Democrats and Republicans. Such groups may come to need each other's distrust. Call this the *irony of the beneficial enemy.*

VIOLATING IDENTIFICATION-BASED TRUST

Trust violations occur when another person's behavior does not conform to expectations.[12] High trust may become low trust, or jump from trust to distrust. Violations of CBT, such as when a dry cleaner overstarches a shirt, have different consequences than violations of IBT, such as when a spouse forgets an anniversary or a manager shames an employee. Violations of CBT may be viewed as merely annoying, depending on the relationship. Though potentially serious, violations of CBT are "not likely to violate our emotional well-being significantly."[13]

Violations of IBT, however, directly impact a person's identity. "The parties are likely to feel upset, angry, violated, or even foolish, if loss of face is a result of trusting the other when trusting turned out to be inappropriate." Lewicki and Wiethoff stress that violations of IBT are far more difficult to address and repair than violations of CBT.[14]

And because IBT fosters *positive emotional attachment*, even to the point where "one party acts for the other even more zealously than the other might demonstrate,"[15] violations of IBT can dras-

---

12. Ibid., 99.
13. Ibid.
14. Ibid.
15. Ibid., 89.

tically impact a wide network of relationships within the group. Many within the group may end up feeling angry and violated. When the regional VP fires a local manager, if the employees reporting to that local manager have positive emotional attachment to her, indicative of high IBT, then their response to her firing may well be stronger and angrier than that of the fired manager herself.

WHEN DISTRUST IS VIOLATED

Distrust can also be violated. CBD can transition to CBT, such as when a once-disappointed patron returns to a restaurant and is pleasantly surprised by the experience. The violation of IBD that results in IBT, however, appears to resonate on a deeper, almost archetypal level. In fact the plots of many movies, including a surprising percentage of Oscar best picture winners—such as *West Side Story*, *Driving Ms. Daisy*, and *Million Dollar Baby*—hinge on this poignant, vulnerable transformation among the main characters. Such examples also reveal how distrust, in any form, is often safer and more instinctive than trust.

TRUST AND VOLUNTARY GROUPS

Many organizations assemble to achieve task goals that require CBT. The shared identity formed within them impacts their culture and performance, but success depends upon getting the job done. A company may well foster the IBT of its clients, but still this IBT is founded upon the company delivering on CB obligations.

In strong contrast, some organizations are made up wholly or largely from volunteers. A PTA, or workers at a soup kitchen, gather according to shared values and interests, increasing the emphasis on IBT. Such groups experience the bonding benefits of IBT, but also navigate the intense challenges brought on when this trust is stretched or violated.

TRUST AND SUBMISSION

One person can submit to another out of either trust or distrust. Trusting submission is voluntary. One party allows the power she has to be employed according to the discretion of another. Examples of trusting submission include a football quarterback running the play called by the coach, and the members of a renowned orchestra playing at the tempo their conductor sets. Trusting submission can also be called **collaborating** or **synergistic submission**, in that it enables a whole to be much more than the sum of the submitting parts. In cases of synergistic submission, one submitting to the leader, e.g. a lead violinist, is often more powerful than the leader in important ways. In other words, the leader may know the one submitting can and will do greater things than the leader. Instances of synergistic submission are also instances of mutual trust and mutual endorsement.

In contrast, submission to a distrusted party is involuntary. Put differently, if you distrust me and I want you to submit, I will likely have to force it. And if I force or demand submission, I will likely earn your increased distrust. This could also be called **forced** or **powerless submission**. This is the submission of inmates to prison guards, and slaves to their masters. Noteworthy is that slavery is far from an archaic example. Roughly thirty million people are enslaved as of late 2013—the highest number in human history.[16] Many of these are children forced into sexual slavery.

---

16. Fisher, "30 Million Slaves, 60,000 in U.S."

What Must I Do . . . ?

To the rich young man running up to Jesus in Mark 10, Jesus may as well be a park ranger, someone who can give him directions. "Good teacher, what must I do to inherit eternal life?"(10:17) This is a religious, calculus-based question, trusting Jesus only for information and obligation. What must this man do to get heaven as compensation? The question is ironic, asking how to earn an inheritance. So Jesus goes along: "You know the commandments . . . "(10:19). Basically, *If you want to do this under your own individual power, try keeping the commandments. See how that goes.*

But Jesus' response begins ironically also: "Why do you call me good? No one is good—except God alone" (10:18). This preface, and likely its relational tone, undermines both the man's question and Jesus' answer. *If you want to know how to be good enough on your own, I'm not a good person to ask.* Still, if this man does not catch his own irony, he will not catch Jesus'. He proudly declares, "All these I have kept since I was a boy" (10:20). His transaction is confirmed. He is good in ways even Jesus will not claim to be.

But, probably in the same way a shepherd looks at and loves a young lamb head-butting his leg, "Jesus looked at him and loved him" (10:21). Jesus continues, "One thing you lack. Go, sell everything you have . . . and come follow me" (10:21). In other words, "Trust me instead of yourself, and don't just trust me but trust in me; identify with me." The young man evidently obeys. That he goes away sad instead of mad implies as much. As he does, an impersonal CBTrust toward Jesus, which is really trust in his own merits, is stretching into a personal faith in him. The relationship will be less about two sides performing as expected, and more about questions like, "Do you love me?" and "Do you know me?" and "Am I safe?" and "Do you still love me?"

Church leaders face the same challenge of encouraging this deeper, more intimate trust in Jesus, and in themselves, in part by stretching that trust. But yes, candidly, a church can survive on mutual CBTrust, with the leader meeting expectations, and depending on those led only to deliver as pledged.

...Because He Is Not One of Us

> "Master," said John, "we saw someone driving out demons in your name and we tried to stop him, because he is not one of us."
> "Do not stop him," Jesus said, "for whoever is not against you is for you." (Luke 9:49–50)

Most organizations rely primarily on CBTrust, the ability to deliver as expected. Churches coalesce around shared IBTrust. Do we identify with each other? Do our values align? But we, like John, can sink to shared IBDistrust. Christians can share the same anxious distrust John boasts, and Jesus corrects. Those not with us must be against us. See how John agrees that Power is at work through this man: he opposes him because *he is not one of us*.

Faith is a risky identity statement. Do I look foolish believing as I do? Am I not ashamed? Christians and churches hold up highly specific identity signs to help address this risk: Missouri Synod, Evangelical, Evangelical Free, full gospel, PCUSA. These communicate shared identity. Can I place IBTrust in this place? Do you identify with me?

The identity risk inherent in faith, unless carefully tended, provides fertile ground for anxiety, which contrives IBDistrust, which looks nothing like faith. Like John, Christians can devoutly oppose different Christians. Marva Dawn's question—"Can we find some way to prevent discussion about worship styles from becoming fierce and bitter battles waged between two entrenched camps?"[17]—reflects the intense trust and distrust dynamics churches negotiate. Church conflicts, especially those involving leadership, are often characterized by the deep, emotional wounds indicative of violated IBTrust. Dynamics like these give many outside The Church ample reason to distrust those within. Church leaders face the same challenge Jesus did, bringing about transformation by addressing the instinctive, anxious IBDistrust John demonstrates.

---

17. Dawn, *Reaching Out Without Dumbing Down*, 3.

...He Became Like One of Us

> When Jesus reached the spot he looked up and said to him, "Zaccheus, come down immediately. I must stay at your house today." (Luke 19:5)

> As he walked along, he saw Levi son of Alphaeus sitting at the tax collector's booth. "Follow me," Jesus told him, and Levi got up and followed him. (Mark 2:11)

Much about the Great Commission places face and identity concerns at risk. The message that I need forgiveness and redemption chafes against my personal and social identity, my desire "be appreciated and approved of,"[18] and my instinct to not be interfered with. This gospel may be Good News at some point, but in the moment I receive it, it can be most unsettling, even offending.

Those within The Church face a dilemma: extend this potentially unwelcome invitation, and risk embarrassment, discomfort, etc. for all parties; or forego the life-giving message of salvation in deference to face and identity concerns.

For his part, Jesus approaches this delicate dilemma with the tact of a 9-month old puppy. He imposes on everyone he meets. To know Jesus is to be put out by him. He invites himself to dinner with tax collectors. He says, "Follow me" without even saying please. He banters with disreputable women. Jesus doesn't mind associating with just about anybody.

Soon or very soon they come to see that associating with him, and trusting him, regardless of the risk, is better than not. Their identities are secure with him, though far from safe. Much imposition and expansion and purpose and power await. Jesus Christ is the most dangerous of leaders. He beckons everyone to enter his Church, but not as a safe destination. As one prophet asks:

> "Safe?" said Mr. Beaver. "Don't you hear what Mrs. Beaver tells you? Who said anything about safe? 'Course he isn't safe. But he's good. He's the King, I tell you."[19]

---

18. Brown and Levinson, *Politeness*, 61.
19. Lewis, *The Lion, the Witch, and the Wardrobe*, 75–76.

CHAPTER 11

Different Forms of Authority

It is not wisdom but authority that makes a law.

—THOMAS HOBBES

Blind belief in authority is the greatest enemy of truth.

—ALBERT EINSTEIN

Authority is one word used to describe many varied forms of power. Looking at words used adjacent to authority—e.g., *given* authority, *an* authority, authority *figure*—helps to diagnose one instance from another. Has someone been *given* authority, for example, meaning another party has designated some form of exclusive, legitimate power to him? Is she called *an* authority, meaning others regard her for her established expertise? Is he described as speaking *with* authority (Greek: *exousia*), meaning others endorse that he communicates with legitimate confidence and evident ability? Or does she merely *exercise* authority (Greek: *exousiazo*) perhaps to bully? Has someone *earned* authority, meaning he has earned high trust, which enables him to correct in ways that stretch that trust? Does he *abuse* authority, meaning he somehow misuses legitimate power for his own gain? Does she act according to her *own* authority, such us as when a company founder gives herself the title of president? Stephen Covey Sr. contributes *natural* authority (power given to humans to steward the rest of creation) and *moral* authority, which describes the reciprocal relationship between a principled leader and principled followers.[1]

Trust-and Distrust-Based Authority

Some forms of authority are trust-based, e.g., testifying as *an* authority, or speaking *with* authority. In contrast, many instances of authority incorporate one or more forms of distrust-based power. Consider how many forms of coercive power a police officer might carry on her belt—gun, taser, mace, stick, radio, handcuffs—and have the legitimate right to use as necessary. As described earlier, coercive power is so closely associated with given authority that the two are often regarded as synonyms, such as when law enforcement agencies are referred to as *the authorities*.

Complicating authority further is that formal leadership positions often are a combination of trust-based authority and distrust-based authority. A professor has *given* authority, but may also be *an* authority, and may *abuse* her authority. Referring to someone as an *authority figure* ascribes to him both high power and the arbitrary potential to act either coercively or benevolently. In what ways does having multiple, varied forms of authority help a leader, and in what ways might it hinder her?

Each of the above examples illustrates something all forms of authority seem to have in common: authority, in whatever form or forms it takes, can trump other forms of power. Other forms of power must adjust to recognized authority. How much, for example, does a domestic violence situation transform when the police arrive? Attorneys on both sides of a trial may appeal vehemently to the judge on a point of trial process, but nod and continue once the judge makes her decision. How authority can overwhelm other forms of power is described later in this chapter, with the connection of authority and face.

---

1. Covey, "Foreword," *The Power of Servant Leadership*. 5.

Is short, authority in any form must be and often is used carefully in leadership settings. Still, these factors complicate but do not negate relational dynamics like endorsement, resistance, and dependence.

GIVEN AUTHORITY

Given authority may be the most recognized form of authority, and possibly the most recognized of all forms of power. "The President of the United States, police, the chairperson of the PTA, the student government leader, your boss at work, all are designated power by their position."[2] Formal leaders are given authority when hired, such as the legitimate power to hire and fire employees, assign responsibilities, etc. *Given* authority is distinct from other forms of authority in several ways, and each suggests strongly that this form of authority belongs to the person *in* authority:

1. Given authority is formally, sometimes ceremoniously endorsed in advance, where other instances of power and authority are endorsed within the interaction. A mayor is sworn in before taking office. A regional director is given her authority when hired to the position. In short, given authority is given.

2. Given authority is often given by people removed from the immediate setting in which the authority is used. A school teacher is given authority by his district. A professional football coach is given authority by the team owner. In contrast, a mayor is elected by a majority of those within that city.

3. Inversely, those directly *under* authority often are not the ones who gave it. Students don't hire their teachers. Prison inmates don't elect their guards.

4. The boundaries of given authority are often very specific. A county sheriff has much authority within his jurisdiction. A basketball referee's whistle has great authority during the game.

---

2. Hocker and Wilmot, *Interpersonal Conflict*, 107.

5. Those with given authority are also recognized for their right to use other forms of power, apart from endorsement, including coercive and even violent power. A state trooper has the right to issue a speeding ticket and even to fire her weapon. She also has the right, as she deems necessary, to exceed the very speed limit she enforces.

Because of these factors and others, given authority—and any other forms of power that accompany this authority role—may well be regarded a possession of the authority figure, and hence not subject to endorsement. A person *given* authority may refer to it as *my* authority. Those under this authority may feel involuntarily dependent on this person (increasing the likelihood of distrust). Contrast this with the person who attempts to possess other forms of authority, for example saying, "I am the authority on this topic" or "I speak with authority." Such statements can be made, but they may well sound pretentious, even arrogant, undermining the trust they are intended to instill. In short, they are still subject to endorsement. (For the record, referring back to Covey's natural authority over creation, anyone who has tried to teach their dog to fetch or tried to keep houseplants alive knows that even natural authority is subject to endorsement. The dog may just look at you. The plants may still die. The saying "You can lead a horse to water but you can't make it drink" reflects this natural truth.)

Even those people under a person's given authority may regard it as *her* authority, especially if they gave it. But at least three general cautions must accompany the perception that given authority belongs to that person it is given to:

First, authority is still subject to ongoing endorsement. "Legitimate power stems from the willingness of others to accept an individual's direction."[3] "Regardless of how tight a hold a party may attempt to have on any resource, the resource is always used in the context of a relationship. It is the other party's view of the resource that makes it a basis for influence."[4] Authority can be resisted, de-

---

3. Vecchio, "Power, Politics, and Influence," 72.
4. Folger et al., *Working Through Conflict*, 146.

nied, or withdrawn. Indeed the United States celebrates every July 4, Independence Day, how it withdrew endorsement of authority previously given. Mayors can be voted out of office. Baseball coaches can be fired. In short, authority given can still be taken away.

Second, endorsement of given authority consists of compliance or obedience only, i.e., meeting some measurable minimum standards. A speed limit sign, for example, tangibly delineates between obedience and disobedience. Given authority can enforce classroom attendance but not classroom achievement. Hence given authority is a useful and necessary but limited form of social power. Many desired outcomes cannot be brought about via authority.

A third caution related to given authority is that it can often be evaded. Put differently, withholding endorsement of given authority can be as simple as not going within that authority figure's jurisdiction. Just don't come around. This caution may be of minimal concern, or even ideal to some authority figures. A prison warden, for example, may tell an inmate he doesn't want to see him again. But to the leader/authority figure who wants to be approachable, this caution may be the most significant.

AUTHORITY OVER FACE: THE MILGRAM EXPERIMENTS

Another ominous caution addresses the potential of settings in which leaders steward both given and expert authority. Stanley Milgram conducted a series of troubling yet fascinating and critically acclaimed experiments, documented in his book *Obedience to Authority*, that consistently demonstrated that average people were easily willing to behave quite coercively, even violently and inhumanely, in obedience to an authority figure.

The experiments were set up to answer the basic question: "How does a man behave when he is told by a legitimate authority to act against a third individual?"[5] Specifically, an individual was assigned by an authority figure—a white-jacketed "experimenter"—

---

5. Milgram, *Obedience to Authority*, 5.

to administer electric shocks to a third individual when that person failed to complete a basic task. (It should be noted that the third individual was an actor. No third individuals were harmed in the conducting of Milgram's experiments.) Individual subjects in a room with an individual experimenter were told by the experimenter to administer shocks in increasing intensity based on the performance of the third individual. In his preface, Milgram asks and answers the reasonable face-related question, "why anyone in his right mind would administer even the first shocks. Would he not simply refuse and walk out of the laboratory? But the fact is no one ever does."[6] Further, "many of the subjects will obey the experimenter no matter how vehement the pleading of the person being shocked, no matter how painful the shocks seem to be, and no matter how much the victim pleads to be let out."[7]

> This is, perhaps, the most fundamental lesson of our study: ordinary people, simply doing their jobs, and without any particular hostility on their part, can become agents in a terrible destructive process. Moreover, even when the destructive effects of their work become patently clear, and they are asked to carry out actions incompatible with fundamental standards of morality, relatively few people have the resources needed to resist authority. A variety of inhibitions against disobeying authority come into play and successfully keep the person in his place.[8]

To anyone incredulous at the subjects' willingness to obey, certain that she would respond differently, Milgram extends stern caution.

> Many of the subjects, at the level of stated opinion feel quite as strongly as any of us about the moral requirement of refraining from action against a helpless victim. They, too, in general terms know what ought to be done and can state their values when the occasion arises. This has little, if anything, to do with their actual behavior

6. Ibid.
7. Ibid.
8. Ibid., 6.

under the pressure of circumstances ... Moral factors can be shunted aside with relative ease by a calculated restructuring of the informational and social field.[9]

From a standpoint of working with distrust-based authority, "Many people were unable to realize their values in action and found themselves continuing in the experiment even though they disagreed with what they were doing."[10] From the standpoint of working with trust-based authority, "[The subjects] want to put on a competent performance, but they show an accompany narrowing of moral concern. The subject entrusts the broader tasks of setting goals and assessing morality to the experimental authority he is serving."[11]

Milgram's research findings speak volumes about how face concerns and relationship goals can skew a person's response within the immediate interaction, and the ways even strongly held identity concerns can be disrupted within authority settings.

WHO GAVE YOU THIS AUTHORITY? 4 SOURCES

A pivotal question within given authority settings is: who is doing the giving? Given authority can be designated from four directions. It can come from those who will be *under* that authority, such as when a city elects a mayor. Authority can be given by those who will be peers, such as when a state medical board grants a license to practice or police cadets are sworn in to the force. Given authority can also be designated by those *over* that authority, such as when a university president hires a head football coach. Finally, ownership allows a person to designate authority to herself, such as when a company founder by *her own authority* names herself president, or when a child appoints himself supreme commander of the cardboard box spaceship he has created.

   9. Ibid., 6–7.
  10. Ibid., 6.
  11. Ibid., 7.

Another key distinction between these four levels of giving is to assess how given authority is *withdrawn* in each. For example, authority designated from above, such as when a VP hires a store manager, might be withdrawn as quickly as that VP saying, "I'm letting you go." Meanwhile, those who work under that manager may have little or no influence. Authority designated by a peer organization, such as when a state health board revokes a doctor's license to practice or a school district dismisses a tenured teacher, is often more far more complicated. It may involve a complaint, review, suspension, and appeal processes. Meanwhile, when authority is given by the majority of those who will be under that authority, such as when a governor is elected, withdrawing that authority will most likely require waiting for the next election. And finally, if someone acts according to *her own authority*, the only way to withdraw endorsement is to leave that setting.

All of these examples help explain how a sense of low power and anxiety can germinate in given authority settings. Do those under that authority feel voluntarily dependent, or trusting, toward that person given authority? Who among them feels involuntarily dependent upon this authority, and hence prone to distrust?

THREE IRONIES OF GIVEN AUTHORITY

Three ironies accompany given authority roles:

Irony 1: Authority is given away as a means of increasing power.

When authority is given, such as when a mayor is elected or a football coach is hired, this is a deliberate process of giving legitimate power away in order to increase one's own power, i.e. to bring about desired outcomes; to live the live I want to live. In giving authority to a federal court judge, for example, those appointing her give to her exclusive power to determine guilt or innocence. I give up the right to *take matters into my own hands*. But I do so to better attain my own goals of peace and safety.

Irony 2: The trusting, collaborative process of giving authority typically results in a relationship undergirded by coercive, distrust-based power.

When a city elects a mayor, the electorate gives that mayor the authority to hire a police chief, who is entrusted with leading others who enforce laws. This is a multistep but straightforward example of how a trusting, collaborating, courtship-like selection process results in the control of distrust-based, violent power. This power is then used on behalf of, and when necessary on, members of the electorate.

Those giving authority often navigate this irony, including the loss of power and the anxiety that results, by establishing processes to withdraw this authority if necessary. Elections are an obvious example. Beyond these, formal processes to remove authority include, for example, performance contracts, conduct clauses, tenure reviews, and probation periods.

Irony 3: Given authority exists to increase the power of the group *under* that authority.

This irony is not the same as the first irony. Others may give me authority, from many directions. But the reason that authority was given is to enable the group assembled under that authority to achieve its purposes.

This is true of any instance of given authority: prison guard, coach, county sheriff, school teacher, or army general. A county sheriff, for example, is given authority to keep the peace, i.e. to help the group within that county to live peacefully. The college football coach may coach individual players, but if the team as a whole fails to win, he should expect to have his authority withdrawn. Prison guards' duties may include catching and punishing individual rule breakers, but this is done foundationally to provide a humane place for the inmate group to serve their time.

That authority figure who views her role solely as control or high power or the right to give orders does not understand the context or purpose of the role. And those under that authority who equate authority solely with control and coercion and involuntary dependence, risk seeing that authority figure solely as someone to distrust and resist.

THAT MOST POWERFUL FORM OF AUTHORITY

All forms of authority, be they trust-based or distrust-based or both, make more sense when brought under one form of authority all leaders should aim for, along with every person responding to that authority. Pastor and Christian author Max Lucado addresses authority in its most artful form, *earned authority*, in advice to church leaders that could be heeded by those with any form of authority in any setting:

> We no longer live in a day in which the pastor is given authority just by virtue of the title. That change is probably good for us. Now we must earn the authority to speak into someone's life.[12]

---

12. Dyck, "Glad You Asked," 3.

Therefore Go ...

> Then Jesus came and said to them, "All authority in heaven and on earth has been given to me." (Matt. 28:18)
>
> "Therefore go and make disciples of all nations, baptizing them in the name of the Father and of the Son and of the Holy Spirit, and teaching them to obey everything I command you. And surely I am with you always, to the very end of the age." (Matt. 28:19–20)

Jesus pointedly fuses his authority given from God with this Commission given to us. With the two words "Therefore go ... " Jesus succinctly illustrates the third irony of given authority: given authority is legitimate power given precisely to increase the power of the group assembled under that authority.

Jesus also succinctly necessitates why Matthew 28:19–20 should never be severed from the context of Matthew 28:18. To do so risks taking something Jesus has obligated himself to, and saying, "we've got it from here." More subtly, it frees me to pursue this purpose for my own ends.

Instead, Jesus firmly rests our power within trusting, synergistic submission to his authority. Paul delineates this balance as well, describing how we are ambassadors conveying the appeal, but it is his appeal. My duty is to implore. We are responsible for the ministry and message of reconciliation, but not for reconciling:

> All this is from God, who reconciled us to himself through Christ and gave us the ministry of reconciliation: that God was reconciling the world to himself in Christ, not counting people's sins against them. And he has committed to us the message of reconciliation. We are therefore Christ's ambassadors, as though God were making his appeal through us. We implore you on Christ's behalf: Be reconciled to God. (2 Corinthians 5:18–20)

From the Bully Pulpit

Most church leaders are not given the formal distrust-based power that often accompanies given authority. Church leaders cannot fire members of the congregation, or reassign them to a different denomination. But informal coercive power is still available to church leaders. A church leader could relationally communicate frustration or impatience or guilt, for example, or convert other trust-based forms of power to coercive purposes.

The concept of the **bully pulpit** is a familiar example of this. The pulpit is, in all ways, an elevated vantage point in congregational life. The temptation and ease around converting it to a platform for coercive power is understandable, especially given that most sermons are passively endorsed. (Indeed, sermons are better platforms of the *lecture hall irony* than the lecture hall.) But, in an interview with John Chandler, Pastor Fred Craddock speaks candidly and thoroughly about resisting the temptation of the bully pulpit for the sake of expansive leadership, empowerment, earned authority and shared identity:

> I have conversations with the congregation at times other than from the pulpit. The pulpit is always a bully pulpit. From the pulpit, I have a kind of home-field advantage-a sort of a 'no talk back' zone ... People need to learn to express with courage. If I have the courage to stand down here and raise a matter, listen to your objections, listen to you in a way that feels the anger of some and support of others, then everybody is growing. If I just "preach on it," then it becomes, "That's what the minister thinks, and I agree or disagree." I never want to put a congregation in that position of just agreeing or disagreeing. There has to be a fuller expression of its ***own*** life.[13]

That growth and fuller expression, as Craddock insists, demands dialogue. Jesus appears to agree with Craddock's assertion, relying as he does on dialogue-based teaching rather than 'no talk back' sermons.

---

13. Chandler, *Courageous Church Leadership*, 30 (emphasis original).

Who Gave You This Authority?

Church leaders face at least three distinct challenges related to given authority. First, most people who are given authority can point to one specific source of their authority. In contrast, church leaders are often given authority by multiple givers. Authority may be seen as given by those *under* that authority (e.g. the hiring congregation, or the lay leadership responsible for hiring), and by someone above and removed from that setting (e.g. a bishop), and by their ordination vows, and by Scripture, and by God.[14] "Who is right?" is one question. But a more practical question is, "Do they all agree?" Often they don't.

In short, of all the settings in which the question "Who gave you this authority?" can be asked, nowhere is more nebulous and contradictory than in a local church. (Maybe this is why Jesus found a clever way to not answer it in Matthew 21.)

Second, most given authority settings have specific perimeters. A referee is done at the end of the game. A police chief has specific jurisdiction. Church leaders are not off duty, or done after clocking out. From another perspective, a city manager can view as much porn as she likes *on her own time*. A church leader found to have pornography on his home computer is likely to have his given authority removed.

Third, most instances of given authority rely upon formal coercive power and calculus-based distrust, such as a judge's authority to issue a bench warrant. No relationship is necessary. Church leaders face the challenge, summed up earlier in the words of Max Lucado, of constantly earning their authority. Earned authority demands a careful, artful, relational blending of identification-based trust and identification-based distrust.

14. Garrison, *Rethinking Church*, 54.

CHAPTER 12

The Ironies of Coercive Power

Coercive power, the ability to bring about outcomes undesired by another, is at or near the root of many power-related power-related ironies, including *the irony of Al Capone* and *the second irony of given authority*. One reason power is often equated with coercion, as chapter 1 describes, is because coercive power can be wildly entertaining. As the centuries-old sports industry attests, the coercion inherent in competition can be appealing to the point of obsession. And this attraction is not limited to sports. Elimination "reality" television contests, dog shows, elections, county fair bake-offs, beauty pageants, and children's spelling bees all leverage the compelling nature of competition. Even Winnie the Pooh and friends are captivated by their game of Pooh sticks.[1]

The appeal of coercive power acknowledged, it might not the main reason power is often equated with coercion. Instead, power is reasonably equated with coercion in part because any other form of power, even trust-based power like expertise, can be converted to coercive power easily. This *irony of converted coercion*, described in chapter 3, is the most basic of the ironies of coercive power: any form of power can be converted to coercive power, and once converted it may be more effective, i.e., more powerful, than that form of power in its pure, original form.

1. Milne, *House at Pooh Corner*, 94.

THE DOUBLE IRONY OF THE COERCIVE LEADER

A leader who relies solely on trust-based forms of power, such as rewards, expertise, and positive communication skills, will lead much differently than a leader who adheres to *the irony of Al Capone*, relying on some balance of trust-and distrust-based power. And those leaders who rely primarily on coercive power, and power-over tactics, face a chorus of caution from scholars of power. Coleman draws upon Deutsch and Kipnis when stating:

> From a practical perspective, a chronic competitive approach to power has harmful consequences. Deutsch (1973) pointed out that the reliance on competitive and coercive strategies of influence by power holders produces alienation and resistance in those subjected to power. This, in turn, limits the power holder's ability to use other types of power based on trust (such as normative, referent, and reward power) and increases demand for scrutiny and control of subordinates ... If the goal of the power holder is to achieve commitment from subordinates (rather than merely short-term compliance) excessive reliance on a power-over strategy eventually proves to be costly as well as ineffective. Research by Kipnis (1976) supported this contention by demonstrating that a leader's dependence on coercive strategies of influence has considerable costs in undermining relationship with followers and in compromising goal achievement.[2]

Recall from chapter 2 that some definitions of power and leadership emphasize relationships and some emphasize goals, and some emphasize both. In polar contrast to all of these, note how a leader depending solely on coercive power has the potential to *undermine relationships* and *compromise goal achievement*—at the same time. Leaders who rely excessively on coercive, win-lose tactics work against every known definition of leadership and every known definition of power. Call this *the 45th irony*, or **the double irony of the coercive leader**.

---

2. Coleman and Deutsch, *Handbook of Conflict Resolution*, 122.

THE IRONIES OF COERCIVE POWER

THE VIOLENT IRONIES

Chapter 4 described how social power, in contrast to individual power, is determined by the endorsement process. Chapter 6 described the ominous, omnipresent exception to this. "Excluding situations of unequal physical power and use of violence, power is a property of the social relationship rather than a quality of the individual."[3] Physical violence is the one form of social power that an individual can *have*—and force upon others—without their agreement. This tangible, inherently coercive and competitive form of power is available to anyone able to use it, including the person who *resorts to violence* when other forms of power are not endorsed. In fact, one appeal of violence is that is simplifies social power by pushing the endorsement process aside.

Any weapon amplifies violent power, be that a wooden stick, a mother's gun in the hands of an angry third grader, a hijacked aircraft, or a three-million-dollar government-contracted, laser-guided air-to-ground missile. Violent power is the power of war and the power that police officers carry to bolster their legitimate power. Those decrying others' use of violent power should assess the many and constant ways they themselves rely upon it. The pervasiveness of this odd form of social power may be the single biggest reason power is under-understood. Hundreds of billions of euros, yuan, dollars, pesos, drachmas, etc. is devoted annually to threaten violent power, on personal, local, state, national, and international levels, mostly in the name of keeping the peace.

The Terrorist Ironies

And violent power, or the threat of it, can be a misguided means to force endorsement of trust-based power. For example, one person may point a gun at another, and demand respect. This is intensely distrust-based power employed the coerce this respect—i.e., "high

---

3. Hocker and Wilmot, *Interpersonal Conflict*, 116.

or special regard: esteem"[4]—but respect is an ongoing endorsement of trust-based power.

The use of violent, distrust-based power to force endorsement of trust-based power is a self-defeating irony that can be named in too many ways, e.g., *the gangster's irony, the bully's irony, the terrorist's irony, the letter bomb irony*. For example, on September 22, 1995, the *Washington Post* printed an article titled "The Unabomber Manifesto." Publishing this declaration was not an endorsement of this person's expertise or referent power, but instead an endorsement of threatened violence.

An extremely counterintuitive form of this irony can be called **the irony of the shy terrorist**. This very specific irony incorporates at least five confounding, contradictory elements:

1. A surprise attack, allowing no opportunity for endorsement,
2. on random victims, including some who may endorse the terrorist's views,
3. using a device that allows that terrorist to be removed from the violence,
4. with the intent to gain as much attention as possible.
5. Meanwhile the terrorist hides and seeks respect.

In fairness to other terrorists, not all fit this description. Some, for example, kill themselves as part of their attack. But some are terrorist *leaders*, ordering others, even children, to attack while they themselves hide and seek respect.

Beyond violence, other forms of overwhelming coercive power—emotional, psychological, professional—can be employed in the attempt to force respect or even admiration from fear. This can happen in the home, on the street, or in the office. *The playground bully's irony* could easily become *the office bully's irony*. The common thread in these ironies is that the threat of distrust-based power is used as a self-defeating means to force endorsement of trust-based power. The bully seeks to force respect instead of

---

4. *Merriam-Webster Online*, "respect," 3a.

meriting it. Unlike the violent ironies, however, these ironies do involve some degree of endorsement.

Nevertheless, despite any ease and appeal and effectiveness of coercive power, we must never allow fear to become synonymous with respect.

Ironies Leaders Navigate

> ### The Turn or Burn Irony
>
> Fortunately the theology and nature of hell are topics well outside the margins of these pages. That said, how Jesus talks about hell, and doesn't, must be examined because he speaks of it coercively. Jesus talks frankly and occasionally about hell. Further, he describes it as an unpleasant destination God has the authority to send people to. But compare the following two coercive admonitions, the former by Jesus and the latter not:
>
>> I tell you, my friends, do not be afraid of those who kill the body, and after that have nothing more they can do. But I will show you whom you should fear: Fear the one who, after the killing, has authority to throw you into hell. Yes, I tell you, fear him! (Luke 12:5-7)
>
>> You're going to hell if you don't accept Jesus.
>
> These coercive statements differ in at least three fundamental ways. First, where Jesus' describes a fearful authority God controls, the latter speaker takes on that authority. This person assumes authority she is not given, much like the person who says God would never send someone to hell. In contrast, Jesus' caution is like the Surgeon General's warning on a pack of cigarettes, or a principal telling students not to even joke about bringing a gun to school. A hospital HR director who details the termination policy during orientation is providing appropriate guidance, not a threat.
>
> Second, where Jesus' coercive caution seeks to instill a legitimate fear, the latter threat attempts to coerce faith. This is calculus-based, distrust-based power employed to force the highest form of identification-based trust. Did Jesus ever attempt this miracle? Call this the turn or burn irony. This is a not-so-distant cousin to the bully's irony.
>
> Finally, the latter threat is aimed at someone who is not yet among The Church, and who does not yet trust Jesus Christ. In keen contrast, when Jesus issues his dread-full caution, he says "my friends." He is "speaking first to his disciples," (See Luke 12:1). In short, he is speaking to his leaders: he is speaking that person making the latter threat above.

The Irony of Malchus' Ear

The most shameful days The Church has endured have been those in which some have taken matters into their own hands, employing coercive, even violent power in faithless, Powerless attempts to achieve the purposes of The Church.

While violence may seem absurd to modern church leaders and others, we must keep in mind that one disciple resorted to it, and more than one wanted to. James and John nominated burning down an inhospitable Samaritan village (Luke 9). Peter deftly cut off a servant boy's ear, in an attempt to accomplish something possibly somehow related to Jesus' arrest (John 18:10).

Something happens before Peter's assault and something happens after, both of which make the setting that much more ironic. First, Jesus has already told the arresting party, which includes a detachment of Roman soldiers, who he is, with powerful effect.

> When Jesus said, "I am he," they drew back and fell to the ground. (John 18:6)

Evidently Jesus can get by without Peter's violent heroics. Second, after Peter attacks the servant boy, Jesus must interrupt his own arrest to repair the damaged ear (Luke 22:51). Call such violence on behalf of The Church **the irony of Malchus' ear**. This irony has tragically occurred on far larger scales, even against entire people groups, and against other parts of The Church. What must Jesus do to repair that damage?

CHAPTER 13

The Ironies of Power Imbalance

> The effect of power and publicity on all men is the aggravation of self, a sort of tumor that ends by killing the victim's sympathies.
>
> —HENRY ADAMS

Leadership settings are often if not always power imbalanced. Such settings can be immensely, synergistically powerful, provided the leader and every one of those he leads share a healthy blend of trust and distrust, and are expecting to endorse one another. Implicit within this statement, however, are several basic reasons power-imbalanced settings often hinder themselves.

THE WANT FOR POWER

Some people have more power than others, for numerous straightforward reasons described across previous chapters. One person may have more expertise than another. The act of giving authority prima facie creates a power imbalance. One person may have exclusive power others don't, and have the technology to amplify that power. A person singing quietly and beautifully on television can captivate people on every continent.

In addition to these mathematical causes of power imbalance, deeper motivational reasons exist. Some people simply want high power. Some people want more power than they currently have. Some people just want enough power to achieve their valued purposes, such as owning a home and raising children. And some people prefer low power, wanting others to have power on their behalf. Any leadership setting may contain all of these. Offered here is a brief sketch of this spectrum.

Some People Want High Power

People who want high power want it for different reasons. McClelland labels an individual's need for power as *nPower*, describing a person with high *nPower* as having a high need for power. Such a person will "experience great satisfaction in influencing other people and arousing strong emotions in them."[1] "Individuals high on *nPower* seek out positions of authority."[2] McClelland also presents two options for why this power is desired. Someone with a **personalized power orientation** is "exemplified by a tendency to dominate others in an attempt to satisfy one's hedonistic desires."[3] Such a person has a chronic competitive disposition. In contrast, a person with high *nPower* and a **socialized power orientation** may use this "for the good of a cause, an organization, or an institution."[4] To be clear, McClelland's self-orientations differ from the other orientations described in chapter 7, which describe possible orientations toward other people's power.

---

1. Coleman and Deutsch, *Handbook of Conflict Resolution*, 117.
2. Ibid.
3. Ibid.
4. Ibid.

Some People Want Enough Power: The FIRO-B

"We each need enough power to live the life we want. We want to influence events that matter to us."[5] But some simply don't want power as much as others want it, in part because the lives they want to live don't require it. Dr. William Schutz's FIRO-B (Fundamental Interpersonal Relations Orientation-Behavior) instrument illustrates this. Specifically, the FIRO-B assessment places respondents along three spectrums, according to *need for control*, *need for inclusion*, and *need for affection*.[6] (All three of these spectrums involve power, most explicitly the control spectrum.) Those with a high need to express control of others, for example, end up near one end of this specific FIRO-B spectrum, and those with a high want to have others control them wind up near the other end. Those who just want enough power, i.e., they don't have a high need to express power or a high want for others to express power over them, end up closer toward the middle.

Some People Want Low Power

> It may be hard for the movers and shakers of this world to understand, but Schutz's FIRO theory recognizes that some people have a desire to be submissive and dependent, to have their paths laid out by others. Viewed negatively, these people with an inclination to empower others can be seen as wimps. A more charitable judgment is that they are trusting, respectful, obedient, and willing to serve.[7]

Some people, at least in certain settings, want to depend upon the power of others. As Schutz describes, one person preferring another have power over him may be regarded, rightly, as respectful, even obedient. Peter Block, however, presents another perspective in his contrast between citizens and consumers. Block refrains

---

5. Hocker and Wilmot, *Interpersonal Conflict*, 104.
6. Griffin, "FIRO Theory of Needs," 94–96.
7. Ibid., 94.

The Ironies of Power Imbalance

from charity as he describes those with an ongoing low power preference, and how they impact community and society:

> [Regarding Citizens] Our definition here is that a citizen is one who is willing to be accountable for and committed to the well-being of the whole. That whole can be a city block, a community, a nation, the earth. A citizen is one who produces the future, someone who does not wait, beg, or dream for the future.
>
> The antithesis of being a citizen is the choice to be a consumer or a client. . . . Consumers give power away. They believe that their own needs can be best satisfied by the actions of others—whether those needs are elected officials, top management, social service providers, or the shopping mall. Consumers allow others to define their needs. If leaders and service providers are guilty of labeling or projecting onto others the "needs" to justify their own style of leadership or service they provide, consumers collude with them by accepting others definition of their needs. This provider-consumer transaction is the breeding ground for entitlement, and it is unfriendly to our definition of citizen and the power inherent in that definition.[8]

Consumers prefer to give power away, and have others exercise power on their behalf. Consumers hear the statement "with great power comes great responsibility," and respond, "Yes, precisely."

Consumers prefer to set expectations and observe, to either worship success or excoriate failure. They contribute by declaring who is to blame, and pride themselves on how adroitly they describe the problem. The consumer brings about her desired outcomes precisely by achieving low power status and dwelling upon others' obligations. Call this **the consumer's irony**. Power-imbalanced settings are ideal for consumers. The overall power of any organization corresponds to that extent to which it caters to those who prefer low power.

However, two cautions must accompany this irony. First, it is a profound fundamental attribution error to assume that those

---

8. Block, *Community*, 63.

with low power prefer it that way. Most don't. (One way to determine whether those with low power actually want low power is to attempt to empower them, or endorse them in some way, and observe their response.) A second caution related to consumers is that those with power, e.g., money, may still want to be consumers. As the very term *consumer* implies, and Block's description alludes to when mentioning shopping malls and elected officials, consumers may be willing to pay money, perhaps much money, to bestow expectations and achieve consumer status.

MINIMUM SYMBIOSIS

Reconsider Block's description of how leaders and consumers collaborate:

> If leaders... are guilty of labeling or projecting onto others the "needs" to justify their own style of leadership..., consumers collude with them by accepting others definition of their needs.[9]

This collaboration resonates with each of McClelland's self-orientations. For the leader with McClelland's *personalized orientation* toward his own power, a power-imbalanced setting is ideal. Such a leader gains power, while consumers give it away and get their needs defined and met. Everybody wins. For that leader with a *socialized power orientation*, who wants power for the good of a cause or organization, this state is less than ideal, but still workable, depending on the leader. The consumers still get what they want and expect, and the leader still furthers the organization's goals. This setting is suitable, perhaps even preferable, for that leader with an insufficient orientation toward those he leads. As Block states, leaders collude with consumers to define what the group considers successful.

While such settings are not necessarily ironic, this cooperation does pull toward a state of **minimum or even destructive symbiosis**, in which leaders and led collaboratively achieve their individual

---

9. Block, *Community*, 63.

THE IRONIES OF POWER IMBALANCE

purposes while the group as a whole erodes. A pure example of such a setting may not exist. Instead, groups usually include at least some besides the leader who want power, and leaders who want to empower, and some who critically assess the group's impact. But such a group is possible. Describing it is merited if only as a caution.

PROBLEMS WITH POWER IMBALANCE

Concepts presented so far in this chapter describe how and why some people might consider power imbalance ideal. But scholars describe in concert how people usually don't. Power-imbalanced settings are problematic for both high-and low-power parties. People with low power usually want and need more, for task and relationship goals, but also for their own identity and face. "When you are low power in a relationship that matters, you may feel a sense of low self-esteem, of feeling worthless or unable to influence your situation. You may feel sad, defeated, or depressed."[10]

Meanwhile, those in high-power positions "often feel burdened with decision-making responsibilities, worry about being blamed, and feel responsible for doing more than is good for them."[11] *The irony of the burdened leader* describes that leader who has high power relative to those she leads but low power relative to her obligations toward them. Such a leader may well feel all of the above.

Metamorphic Effects of High Power

High power parties may experience what Kipnis calls "metamorphic effects of power."[12] These include acquiring a taste for power, "devaluation of the target person's abilities," enhanced self-perception "so that he views himself more favorably than the target

---

10. Hocker and Wilmot, *Interpersonal Conflict*, 126.
11. Ibid.
12. Ibid.

person," and preferring to "maintain a social and psychological distance from the target person."[13]

Keltner's more recent research, described in *The Power Paradox*, agrees with Kipnis' conclusions, even to the point of irony:

> Lord Acton's thesis has now been tested in hundreds of scientific studies, documenting what brief shifts in power do to our patterns of thought and action... The experience of power destroys the skills that gained us power in the first place. In these findings the power paradox strikes us with full force: the very practices that enable us to rise in power vanish in our experience of power.[14]

POWER IMBALANCE AND TRUST

If you have more power than I do, but I trust you, then I believe I am more powerful because of your power.

But if you as a leader begin to use your high power in ways I see as harmful to my interests, perhaps initiating some change I don't agree with, I may reasonably transition to a distrusting, competing orientation, compounded by a sudden concern that you have more power than I have. Further, if this transition is accompanied by a sense of violated identification-based trust, then this change will be complicated by high emotions and sense of betrayal. In short, power-imbalanced settings can go from highly cooperative to anxious and emotionally competing in the time it takes to change perceptions. For leaders, many *honeymoon periods* end this way. "People who are convinced they have little influence and who are threatened are more likely to commit acts of desperation."[15] One challenge leaders face is establishing identification-based trust before leading others where they might not want to go, and tending to that trust during that change.

---

13. Kipnis, *Powerholders*, 168–78.
14. Keltner, *The Power Paradox*, pp. 99–100.
15. Folger et al., *Working Through Conflict*, 165.

BALANCING POWER IMBALANCE

Scholars describe several means to adjust power imbalance, both formal and informal, and both constructive and destructive to the group. A low-power party can, for example, reduce dependence upon a high-power party or even end the relationship if the dependence allows. She can also adjust her goals that relate to the high-power party, including their identity goals. A person who says her job "pays the bills" may rely on that job to achieve task goals only, but have little or no investment in company culture. A low-power party can offset power imbalance by expanding other available sources of power. The family systems concept of triangulation, in which two parties identify with each other around their assessment off a third party, is a straightforward informal means to expand interpersonal linkage power. An example of formally increasing power is trade workers forming a union. The high level of identification-based trust common among union members, and the dynamics this trust fosters, also merit note.

A shared sense of low power is a compelling common issue around which to form a collective identity, and the kindling for numerous uprisings throughout history, such as the French Revolution and the Boston Tea Party. These examples illustrate a familiar, drastic means of balancing power which low power parties often resort to, actually working to destroy the leadership setting "as the ultimate move to bring about a balance of power."[16]

High-power parties also have many means to balance power for the sake of the group, all of which demand increased trust. They can increase dependence on low-power parties, for example, by endorsing and delegating. This implies that those low-power parties must be seen as, or must become, dependable. Leaders can also refrain from using certain forms of power available to them, though a question must accompany this step: Is the overall power of the group reduced by doing this?

Balancing power by expanding the power of others is also an option. Formal empowerment initiatives may serve this purpose,

---

16. Hocker and Wilmot, *Interpersonal Conflict*, 129.

though these will succeed only if accompanied by endorsement. In fact authentic endorsement, such as listening and respecting and trusting, must remain the architecture for any form of empowerment, formal or informal. "Face to face conversation remains the starting point for enacting the internal desire to balance power."[17] Endorsement, agreeing that someone has power, will always be the foundational element within true empowerment.

However, while leaders stand to gain much power through endorsing and expanding the power of those they lead, some don't, for numerous practical, instinctive reasons.

WHY LEADERS DON'T ENDORSE

A leader endorsing the power of those led increases the power of the leader. This said, the study of power reveals several instinctive, practical reasons for why a leader might not endorse, or might even resist endorsing, those he leads. Listing these often unconscious tendencies serves as a cautionary—if glass-half-empty—summary of this book. Possible reasons a leader would not endorse those he leads include:

- No awareness that endorsement is necessary. For many reasons, including not understanding the relational nature of power, or equating individual power with social power, the leader may see no need to endorse.

- No need. Depending on the leader's goals, she may simply not need power from those she leads. A museum curator may value her benefactors' donations, not their abilities.

- A comparing orientation. The leader may prefer the power imbalance from a relational perspective. "High power is often a goal people strive for."[18]

- A competing orientation. The leader perceives that if another's power increases, her own has decreased.

17. Ibid., 134.
18. Ibid., 127.

The Ironies of Power Imbalance

- A chronic competitive disposition. The leader sees any increased power in others as cause for concern. This leader generally distrusts those he leads.
- A collaborating orientation: Another person's power is fine, and even good, but not essential.
- An insufficient orientation: The low-power party is not expected to have power to endorse. "We endorse those we expect to be powerful and do not endorse those we expect to be weak."[19]
- Leader's sense of low power: A leader burdened by expectations and needing endorsement herself may well resist endorsing others, in part because this endorsement may well burden her more.
- Specific identity and face concerns: The leader may see the endorsement of others as an imposition, or as something contrary to the public image she wants others to have of her. Such a leader may prize a reputation for being distant, gruff, or *stingy with compliments*.
- Too busy. Fiske describes leader's potential to become "attentionally overloaded."[20] A burdened leader may simply not have the time, focus or energy to empower others.
- No means to control the empowered state: the leader may sense that the other's goals—task, relational, identity or face—may be problematic, or that the empowered party may simply get out of control. This concern may stem from the leader's lack of established distrust-based power. Will he be able to *rein her in* if her new power *goes to her head*?

---

19. Folger et al., *Working Through Conflict*, 143.
20. Fiske, "Controlling Other People," 621.

Ironies Leaders Navigate

THE IRONY OF HENRY V

The previous chapter described how, as power imbalance increases, face threat increases. "The greatest potential face threat is found when there is great social distance between the parties, the listener has more power than the speaker, and there is a great degree of imposition placed on the communicative request or act."[21] A leader's high power is face threatening, causing those led to be more guarded and less likely to be authentic.

But what if authenticity is precisely what the leader is seeking? The increased face threat that comes with increased power imbalance stands squarely against that leader with relationship goals like friendship, camaraderie, and *give and take*. What about the leader who desires community, or intimacy in the form of frank honesty? One ironic option, demonstrated in the reality series *Undercover Boss*, is for a leader to actually hide her power in order to achieve her relationship goals. Often this means literally and figuratively hiding her face. Call this **the irony of Henry V**, after the king in Shakespeare's play who seeks honesty from commoner members of his army. In Act 4, Scene 1 of this play, Henry covers his head and face under a borrowed cloak, and lies when asked his name. Then he gets almost more than he bargained for. Henry engages in an existential argument over the responsibility the king has for the souls of his soldiers. Together they dissect the king's character, with even Henry questioning the king's integrity. The conversation ends with King Henry being slapped across the face for dishonoring the king. Shakespeare orchestrates an instance of both situational and dramatic irony.

In hiding his face, Henry seeks to relate with those he leads as they would if they were not dependent on him. In short, he lies to gain complete honesty. Does he have this right, even with his own troops? Is he lying to them, or is he honoring them? Can Henry's actions be defended as hiding the truth to obtain truth, like Stanley Milgram did when using actors faking electric shocks to gauge subjects' response to authority? Do Henry's good intentions justify

---

21. Folger et al., *Working Through Conflict*, 175.

the deception? If his men found out about this, would this increase or decrease their trust in him?

Regardless, Henry makes a counterintuitive, ironic decision. He hides his own immense power to bring about the relational outcomes he desires most: candid, heart-felt, non-threatened community.

Where are you?

The irony of Henry V portrays a king hiding his power to achieve delicate relational purposes. God shares Henry's want for authentic, voluntary intimacy. But as Creator, God's challenge extends well beyond that of Henry V and the Undercover Boss. They can just disguise themselves. To foster this same freedom, without deception, might a Creator need to create plausibility that this Creator might not be; that creation created itself?

Much good science contrasts, and many would say contradicts, the creation story. Is this an either/or situation? Or do Genesis 1 and 2 just poetically sketch God's early artistic works?

Beneath this debate, however, deeper ecological power questions await. Why create this debate? Why incorporate so much to indicate this world could have created itself? Why not just create the science to prove overwhelmingly that you are the Creator?

Henry V might answer these questions with others. What if an omnipotent Creator made himself inescapable? What if we unearthed this specific God? Would camaraderie, trust, comfort, give and take, humor—in a word, love—evolve? Or instead might eternity be marked by the same shame and distrust Adam exhibits toward God early in Genesis 3, upon grasping the knowledge of good and evil:

> [But] the Lord God called to the man, "Where are you?"
> He answered, "I heard you in the garden, and I was afraid because I was naked; so I hid." (Genesis 3:9–10)

We now share this knowledge, and Adam's incapacity for it. We shape this world with it. This knowledge sees others' power as a threat. If an omni-potent God made himself undeniable, how would we respond? Like Adam, with shame and distrust? Even if we got to know this creator, would we be at ease? Or would God be someone to honor, place expectations upon, and avoid? In this light, how carefully must God make himself known, so that those he so loves can still have the freedom to choose to love him?

The Double Irony of the Institutional Church

Churches, like The Church, are power-imbalanced leadership settings. In local churches, this imbalance is often ingrained in organization and structure, especially worship. Relational statements like titles, clothing, and the leader's name on the church's street sign reinforce this imbalance, both interpersonally and at a distance. These factors help explain why churches are often called benevolent dictatorships. Leadership may see this, rightly, as symbolic and sacramental. Members may see themselves, and want to, from a low-power perspective, as "trusting, respectful, obedient, and willing to serve."[22] Further, a person wanting high power in a task-focused business setting may come into church, where identity change and identity risk are emphasized, welcoming this low power, consumer status.

But these attributes describe *large power-distance* settings. "In large power distance work situations, the power of an organization is centralized at the upper-management level. Subordinates expect to be told what to do, and the ideal boss plays the benevolent autocrat role."[23] Jesus, in contrast, models *low-power distance* leadership. He prefers dialogue, always sitting down to preach. He likes to answer and ask questions. His followers, whom he calls friends, routinely argue with him. He elevates children and women. He binds his authority to purposes his followers are to achieve. All this helps foster shared identity, high mutual power, high trust, healthy distrust, and high inter-dependence.

Jesus establishes a small power-distance culture contrasting the surrounding large power-distance culture. In ironic response, local churches often establish large power-distance cultures contrasting the surrounding small power-distance culture. Further, where the climactic event for The Church is its Leader actively endorsing and sending out the many, the climactic event in the local church is too often the many coming in to passively endorse its leader. Call these ***institutional church ironies***.

---

22. Griffin, "FIRO Theory of Needs," 94–96.
23. Hofstede Center, "Power Distance Dimensions."

> ### Feed my sheep ...
>
> > As a pastor, you wear many hats and have many 'bosses.' On a given week you may be the preacher, consoler, building-contractor, janitor, personnel manager, counselor, project organizer, mediator, fund-raiser, vision-caster, and peacekeeper. No pastor can always "perform well" in even half of these areas.[24]
>
> Returning to this at once realistic and unrealistic job description, is this a high or low power position? Could expansive, endorsing roles like *coach* and *mentor* and *encourager* be added, and when?
>
> Sheep are not powerful animals, but that's not what Jesus is talking about. This metaphor portrays the dutiful love of the Shepherd, our need for sustenance, and our tendency to stray. However, when naming his followers' capacity for power and Power, Jesus chooses other metaphors, like *salt of the earth* and *city on a hill* and *light of the world*, and non-metaphors like *disciple* and *peacemaker* and *witness* and *servant*. In short, Jesus addresses all his followers as leaders. Church leaders face the challenge of fostering and endorsing this daring, citizenly identity.
>
> But that church leader with an insufficient orientation, who regards those he leads primarily as sheep, risks seeing them as objects of Jesus' affection, but not as fellow ambassadors, perhaps gifted in ways he isn't. She risks not discerning and authentically endorsing what God wants to do, and is doing, through them.
>
> This leader may merely resist those needing identity change, i.e. like Peter and James and John. She risks not preparing them for and diligently escorting them through this change, despite the power, humility, and purpose it instills. Eventually, he risks accumulating a flock of domesticated sheep, and working to do what the flock expects of him. Finally, such a leader risks missing the earnest joy Jesus felt at proclaiming *blessed are you* and *never have I seen such faith* and *you are not to be like that* and *you will do greater things than I* and *Go*.
>
> 24. Slagle, "Three Irrational Beliefs"

Whom the Father Will Send in My Name

> And a voice from heaven said, "This is my Son, whom I love; with him I am well pleased." (Matthew 3:17)

> "Abba, Father," he said, "everything is possible for you. Take this cup from me. Yet not what I will, but what you will." (Mark 14:36)

> "All this I have spoken while still with you. But the Advocate, the Holy Spirit, whom the Father will send in my name, will teach you all things and will remind you of everything I have said to you." (John 14:26)

The Trinity has long perplexed theologians, preachers, and Sunday School teachers. Who came up with it, and why?

Doctrinal quandaries aside, a three-in-one God performs at least one practical, basic service. The Trinity shows us the ropes. We glimpse the culture of heaven. In academic terms, they model the normative reality of redeemed, eternal communion with God. They invite us to Church.

They just get along. They loudly endorse each other. For those used to approaching heaven cerebrally, this may all look too lovey-dovey. Here is a father who openly gushes about his son. Here is a grown son who resolves to obey "daddy," knowing full well this will destroy him. Here is the Spirit, an Advocate the Son promises the Father will send in the Son's name, to Help everyone choosing to join this parade.

Then, after these three model what is normal and exemplary, they invite us to participate in this most non-competitive reality show:

> "As the Father has loved me, so have I loved you. Now remain in my love." (John 15:9)

> "My command is this: love each other as I have loved you." (John 15:12)

Bibliography

Ashforth, Blake E., and Fred A. Mael. "The Power of Resistance: Sustaining Valued Identities," In *Power and Influence in Organizations*, edited Robert M. Kramer and Margaret A. Neale, 89–119. London: Sage, 1998.

Bass, Bernard. "Concepts of Leadership." In *Leadership: Understanding the Dynamics of Power and Influence in Organizations*, edited by Robert P. Vecchio, 3–22. 2nd ed. Notre Dame: University of Notre Dame Press, 2008.

Blanchard, Kenneth, and Spenser Johnson. *The One Minute Manager*. New York: Berkley, 1998.

Block, Peter. *Community: The Structure of Belonging*. San Francisco: Berrett-Koehler, 2009.

Brainyquote.com. "Albert Einstein Quotes." Online: http://www.brainyquote.com/quotes/authors/a/albert_einstein.html.

———. "Alexander Solzhenitsyn Quotes." Online: http://www.brainyquote.com/quotes/authors/a/alexander_solzhenitsyn.html.

———. "John C. Maxwell Quotes." Online: http://www.brainyquote.com/quotes/authors/j/john_c_maxwell.html.

———. "Leonardo da Vinci Quotes." Online: http://www.brainyquote.com/quotes/authors/l/leonardo_da_vinci.html.

———. "Lord Acton Quotes." Online: http://www.brainyquote.com/quotes/authors/l/lord_acton.html.

———. "Napoleon Bonaparte Quotes." Online: http://www.brainyquote.com/quotes/authors/n/napoleon_bonaparte.html.

———. "William Gaddis Quotes." Online: http://www.brainyquote.com/quotes/authors/w/william_gaddis.html.

Bibliography

Braun, Eduardo P. "It's the Culture, Stupid." *Huffington Post*, June, 2013. Online: http://www.huffingtonpost.com/eduardo-p-braun/its-the-culture-stupid_2_b_3487503.html.

Brown, Penelope, and Stephen Levinson, *Politeness: Some Universals in Language Usage*. Cambridge: Cambridge University Press, 1987.

———. Email interview with author, October 2013.

Chandler, John P. *Courageous Church Leadership*. St. Louis: Chalice, 2007.

Coleman, Peter. "Power and Conflict." In *The Handbook of Conflict Resolution*, edited by P. T. Coleman et al., 108–30. 2nd ed. San Francisco: Jossey Bass, 2006.

Collins, Jim. "Level 5 Leadership: The Triumph of Humility and Fierce Resolve." In *Leadership: Understanding the Dynamics of Power and Influence in Organizations*, edited by Robert Vecchio, 394–406. 2nd ed. Notre Dame, IN: University of Notre Dame Press, 2008.

———. "Why Business Thinking Is Not the Answer." Text excerpts from *Good to Great and the Social Sectors*. Author's Note. November 2005. Online: http://www.jimcollins.com/books/g2g-ss.html.

Covey, Stephen, Sr. "Foreword." In *The Power of Servant Leadership*, by Robert Greenleaf. 25th. Anniversary Edition. New York: Paulist, 2002.

Crouch, Andy. *Playing God: Redeeming the Gift of Power*. Downers Grove, IL: InterVarsity, 2013.

Dawn, Marva. *Reaching Out without Dumbing Down*. Grand Rapids: Eerdmans, 1995.

Deutsch, Morton. *The Resolution of Conflict*. London: Yale University Press, 1973.

Duin, Janet. *Quitting Church: Why the Faithful Are Fleeing and What to Do about It*. Grand Rapids: Baker, 2008.

Dyck, Drew. "Glad You Asked: Max Lucado on the Power of Questions, Pastoral Authority, and Giving a Firm Word of Correction." *Leadership Journal*, Summer 2011, 3. Online: http://www.christianitytoday.com/le/2011/summer/gladyouasked.html.

Fisher, Max. "This Map Shows Where the World's 30 Million Slaves Live. There are 60,000 in the U.S." *Washington Post*, October 17, 2013. Online: http://www.washingtonpost.com/blogs/worldviews/wp/2013/10/17/this-map-shows-where-the-worlds-30-million-slaves-live-there-are-60000-in-the-u-s/.

Fiske, Susan. "Controlling Other People: The Impact of Stereotyping." *American Psychologist*, June 1993. Online: http://www.radford.edu/~jaspelme/_private/gradsoc_articles/stereotypes%20and%20prejudice/Power_and_stereotypes.pdf.

Folger, Joseph P., Marshal Scott Poole, and Randall K. Stutman. *Working Through Conflict*. 6th ed. New York: Pearson, 2009.

Forsyth, Donelson. *Group Dynamics*. 5th ed. Belmont, CA: Cengage, 2009.

Foster, Richard. *The Celebration of Disipline:The Path to Spiritual Growth*. San Francisco: HarperCollins, 1998.

———. *The Challenge of the Disciplined Life: Christian Reflections on Money, Sex & Power*. San Francisco: HarperCollins, 1985.
Frazee, Randy. *The Connecting Church*. Grand Rapids: Zondervan, 2001.
Garrison, Becky. *Rising from the Ashes: Rethinking Church*. New York: Church Publishing, 2007.
Greenleaf, Robert. *The Power of Servant Leadership*. San Francisco: Berrett-Koehler, 1998.
———. "The Servant as Leader." In *Leadership: Understanding the Dynamics of Power and Influence in Organizations*, edited by Robert P. Vecchio, 407–15. 2nd ed. Notre Dame: University of Notre Dame Press, 2008.
Griffin, Em. "FIRO Theory of Needs of William Schutz." In *A First Look at Communication Theory*. New York: McGraw-Hill. Online: http://www.afirstlook.com/docs/firo.pdf.
Hawkins, Greg, and Cally Parkinson. *Follow Me: What's Next for You?* Barrington, IL: Willow Creek Association, 2008.
Heartquotes.net. "Leadership Quotes and Proverbs." Online: http://www.heartquotes.net/Leadership.html.
Heath, Anthony. *Rational Choice and Social Exchange: A Critique of Exchange Theory*. London: Cambridge University Press, 1976.
Hocker, Joyce. Email interview with author, April, 2011.
Hocker, Joyce, and William Wilmot. *Interpersonal Conflict*. 9th ed. New York: McGraw-Hill, 2013.
———. *Interpersonal Conflict*. 3rd ed. Dubuque, IA: Wm C. Brown, 1993.
The Hofstede Center. "Power Distance Dimensions." Online: http://geert-hofstede.com/dimensions.html.
Isitironic.com. "Examples of Irony." Online: http://www.isitironic.com/ironiqs.htm.
Johnson, Richard R. "The Psychological Influence of the Police Uniform." 2nd section. Online: http://www.policeone.com/police-products/apparel/undergear/articles/99417-The-psychological-influence-of-the-police-uniform/.
Keltner, Dacher. *The Power Paradox*. New York: Penguin Press, 2016.
King, Martin Luther, Jr. "On Power and Love." Online: http://www.terraquote.com/tag/power-and-love/.
Kipnis, David. *The PowerHolders*. Chicago: University of Chicago Press, 1979.
Kruse, Kevin. "100 Best Quotes on Leadership." *Forbes.com*. Online: http://www.forbes.com/sites/kevinkruse/2012/10/16/quotes-on-leadership/.
Levinger, Gordon. "The Development of Perceptions and Behavior in Newly Formed Social Power Relationships." In *Studies in Social Power*, edited by Dorwin Cartwright, 83–98. Ann Arbor, MI: University of Michigan Press, 1959.
Lewicki, Roy J., and Carolyn Wiethoff. "Trust, Trust Development, and Trust Repair." In *The Handbook of Conflict Resolution*, edited by Peter T. Coleman et al., 86–107. San Francisco: Jossey Bass, 2006.
Lewis, C. S. *The Lion, the Witch and the Wardrobe*. New York: Macmillan, 1970.

Bibliography

———. *Surprised by Joy*. Orlando, FL: Harcourt, 1955.
McKinney, Michael. "The Art of Leadership." *Leading Blog*. Online: http://www.leadershipnow.com/leadingblog/2011/09/the_art_of_leadership.html.
———. "Leadership Quotes." *Leading Blog*. Online: http://www.leadershipnow.com/leadingblog/leadershipquotes.html.
Menconi, Peter. *The Intergenerational Church: Understanding Congregations from WWII to WWW.com*. Littleton, CO: Mt. Sage, 2010.
Milgram, Stanley. *Obedience to Authority—an Experimental View*. New York: Harper & Row, 1974.
Milne, A. A. *The House at Pooh Corner*. New York: Dutton, 1942.
Psychology and Society. "Fundamental Attribution Error." Online: http://www.psychologyandsociety.com/attributionerror.html.
Rowling, J. K. *Harry Potter and the Order of the Phoenix*. New York: Scholastic, 2003.
Scazzero, Peter, with Warren Bird. *The Emotionally Healthy Church: A Strategy for Discipleship that Actually Changes Lives*. Grand Rapids: Zondervan, 2010.
Senge, Peter M. *The Fifth Discipline: The Art & Practice of the Learning Organization*. New York: Currency Doubleday, 1990.
Sjogren, Steve. "Tea With Drucker." *ChurchPlanting.com*. Online: http://www.churchplanting.com/tea-with-drucker/?doing_wp_cron=1507599496.717756032943725585937 5#.Wdwki2hSzIU
Slagle, David. "Three Irrational Beliefs." *Leadershipjournal.net*. Online: http://www.christianitytoday.com/le/2011/summer/irrationalbeliefs.html
Steinke, Peter L. *How Your Church Family Works: Understanding Congregations as Emotional Systems*. Herndon, VA: Alban Institute, 1999.
Ting-Toomey, Stella, and Leeva C. Chung. *Understanding Intercultural Communication*. Los Angeles: Roxbury, 2005.
Tzu, Sun. *The Art of War*. Translated by Lionel Giles. 1910. Reprint, Franklin, TN: Dalmation, 2011.
Ury, William, Jeanne M. Brett, and Stephen B. Goldberg. *Getting Disputes Resolved: Designing Systems to Cut the Costs of Conflict*. San Francisco, Jossey-Bass, 1988.
Vecchio, Robert. "Introduction and Overview." In *Leadership: Understanding the Dynamics of Power and Influence in Organizations*, edited by Robert P. Vecchio, 1–2. 2nd ed. Notre Dame: University of Notre Dame Press, 2008.
———. "Power, Politics, and Influence." In *Leadership: Understanding the Dynamics of Power and Influence in Organizations*, edited by Robert P. Vecchio, 69–95. 2nd ed. Notre Dame: University of Notre Dame Press, 2008.
Weber, Max. *On Charisma and Institution Building*. Edited by S. N. Eisenstadt. Chicago: University of Chicago Press, 1977.

www.ingramcontent.com/pod-product-compliance
Lightning Source LLC
Chambersburg PA
CBHW050821160426
43192CB00010B/1842